MW00364167

Sailors test the wind, while the wind is testing them. You struggle to read wind and wave as you are buffeted, veering, yawing, praying with sail and tiller. In this account of life change, Peter Ilgenfritz doesn't hug the shore, but sets out to be tested. Why does he need to escape the good life he has created by middle age, leaving his successful job, long relationship, and a known identity behind? Simple: his formation requires it. So he sets sail. And in this book, as you leave the shore with this pilot, you may remember your own oblique dreams that summon you out to a deeper life of your own.

—Kim Stafford, author of *Wild Honey, Tough Salt*

Testing the Wind

by Peter Ilgenfritz

cp

coffeetownpress

Kenmore, WA

coffeetown**press**

A Coffeetown Press book published by Epicenter Press

Epicenter Press
6524 NE 181st St. Suite 2
Kenmore, WA 98028.
www.Epicenterpress.com
www.Coffeetownpress.com
www.Camelpress.com

For more information go to: www.epicenterpress.com
Author Website: www.PeterIlgenfritz.com

All rights reserved. No part of this book may be reproduced or transmitted in any form or by any means, electronic or mechanical, including photocopying, recording, or any information storage and retrieval system, without permission in writing from the publisher.

Some of the names of individuals and identifying details cited in this book have been changed to protect their privacy.

Poems in this book were written by Peter Ilgenfritz.

This is a work of nonfiction.

Testing the Wind
Copyright © 2021 by Peter Ilgenfritz

ISBN: 9781603812788 (trade paper)
ISBN: 9781603812795 (ebook)

Printed in the United States of America

To all of my instructors who time and again helped me step off the dock and learn to sail.

Table of Contents

Prologue

There are so many things
I do not want to remember,
and this I do:
how I crouched
on warm beach sand,
by the edge of dark tide pool rocks,
and heard the barnacles crackling,
this opening
to life.

A cold blustery day in mid-October 2013. A small wooden sailboat tips in the wind over a whitecapped lake. Someone on board is yelling, a frantic cry that echoes across the water, "Are you sure? Are you sure this is alright?"

On the south side of Lake Union, the Seattle skyline is punctuated by a dozen orange construction cranes as a new city rises from cavernous holes where redbrick storefronts and Craftsman houses once stood. The Space Needle, just off the southwest corner of the lake has, like me, just marked its fiftieth year. To the East, the brownstone edifice of St. Mark's Cathedral looms over the top of Capitol Hill, the great stained-glass window like a giant eye watching over the changes of a city on the move. My own church, where I've been pastor for some twenty years, is hidden behind the hills to the north.

Today, I see none of these familiar sights. All I see are the churning whitecaps below as we rise higher and higher above the waves. I don't hear the traffic on I-5 murmuring above, the seaplane propellers roaring, or the coxswain on the University of Washington crew team calling out the strokes. All I hear is someone on our boat yelling louder still, "Are you sure? Are you really sure this is alright?"

Sailing's the last thing I thought I'd ever do. Although I've spent most of my life near the sea, growing up on the North Shore of suburban Boston in the 1960's and 70's and here in Seattle for the past two decades, I've never been interested in boats or being out on the water. I've never liked tippy things like roller coasters or skateboards. I especially don't like wind. The howling and flapping of wind, the kind of wind that we're having today, spitting rain from sheets of gray clouds that scurry across a dark sky.

But a few months ago, I started thinking about what I might do on my sabbatical this coming winter when I'd have three months away from the church. I thought about all the familiar things I'd done on previous sabbaticals — trips to see family and friends, a study program abroad. And then I dreamt one night of me at the helm of a thirty-foot sailboat in the South Pacific, cresting the waves in a rolling blue sea. Behind me palm trees tossed in the breeze on white sandy beaches. The sun shone bright overhead. Nothing about the dream felt like me or anyone I'd ever wanted to be. Instead, it felt like a dream that had ended up in the wrong person's imagination. I didn't tell anyone about it.

However, last month, in early September, I'd run into a friend at a wedding reception. I don't know why I told him. Perhaps it was the warm summer day, the glass of champagne in my hand, the relief of my official responsibilities now complete. He asked me what I was thinking of doing on my sabbatical that winter. I told him the kind of things I imagined middle-aged pastors might do — read, write, relax, travel.

Then, I don't know why, I told him about the dream I'd had of me on a sailboat.

"You've got to do it!" he exclaimed.

"But it makes no sense," I shot back, "I've never been interested in boats. I don't like anything about boats."

"It doesn't matter that it doesn't make sense, Peter, it's fun!"

Fun? 'Fun' felt like the last reason I'd want to learn to sail.

As he took off, he called back to me, "The Center for Wooden Boats on Lake Union has sailing classes coming up this fall. Check it out!"

Back on the boat, I grip the side and lean back as far as I dare, trying to drive the boat down flat again on the water. My feet slip on the wet floorboards and someone yells again, his voice constricted in a high-pitched squeak, "We're going over!"

I know that voice. It's mine. Wide-eyed and heart pounding, I feel myself tossed forward, face down in the cold waves, feet tangled in ropes, sails wet and heavy pushing me farther and farther down into the murky water. My chest clenches. *I can't breathe — I'm going to drown!*

"We're fine," I hear my instructor say calmly, "we have a five-hundred-pound keel under us."

I have no idea what a keel looks like. I wonder if it can break or fall off.

I remember a late October afternoon thirty years ago. The sun broke in and out of the clouds casting long shadows over the floor of our freshman seminar class. I looked out the tall windows at the gray bare-branched tree limbs. A few brown leaves still clung to the branches. Dark clouds whisked across the sky. A few flakes of snow. Professor R.V. Smith, stood in the center aisle, looking at us over the top of his reading glasses. He read a few lines from H. Richard Niebuhr's book *Radical Monotheism and Western Culture*. I wrote the lines I remembered in my journal that night:

"There is something about reality with which we all must reckon. We might not be able to give a name to it, calling it only the void out of which everything comes and to which everything returns. Against it, there is no defense."

As I looked down into the churning waves, I felt my whole life falling into that void. I'd just left the comfortable familiarity of a twenty-five-year relationship with a wonderful man who I'd fallen in love with at divinity school, the first and only love in my life. I'd walked away from our beautiful brightly painted condominium on Capitol Hill and moved into a rented room in a faded brown carpeted house with half a closet full of clothes and three cardboard boxes of old journals stuffed under my bed.

I'd had it all once, or so it seemed — a loving relationship, a challenging meaningful job as a pastor at a large urban congregation, a close family, and good friends. But I had something else as well: a weight that sat heavy on my chest, stifling and cold, keeping me from taking a deep breath. I felt like I was being pursued by something behind me, just over my shoulder, but every time I turned to face it, nothing was there. It felt like something wanted to come to life in me or take my life away. Perhaps both. I was terrified of discovering what it was, but I knew it might cost me my life if I did not.

Years ago, shortly after coming to Seattle, I visited an elderly woman who was dying. Always frail, she was all the smaller, frailer. She looked almost as if she were disappearing into the white sheets and pillow. As I sat at her bedside, holding her hand, she opened her blue eyes one last time, tried to smile. Then a pained expression.

"I guess I never really learned who I am," she said.

I don't remember what I said. I hope I held her hand, nodded, showed her that I cared, understood. I did understand, all too well. Her husband was a brilliant extroverted man, strong-willed and opinionated. He'd held lots of fancy positions. She'd supported him, raised the kids. But who she was, herself, she didn't know.

I knew I could be her. Like her, I'd been there for others all my life — as son, brother, uncle, pastor, spouse, foster dad. I knew how to go along, get along. I knew how to be there for others. But I didn't know who I was. I imagined, even longed for, something that I wondered if I could ever let myself have — my own little place on a hill to look out and see my life. It felt wrong, selfish to want something that would cause so much pain to so many I loved. And it also felt so necessary to discover the 'I' of whoever 'I' was. I could never have anticipated that I would find that place years later, not on a lonely hillside but out on a little boat.

To leave Dave and what had been my life in order to discover myself was the hardest and scariest thing I could imagine doing. For months I locked myself deeper and deeper into despair until the night I stood in the bedroom door, Dave sitting on the green patchwork bedspread my mother had quilted for us, his head in his hands.

"I need to go," I said, "I must. And if I don't go now I never will."

Walking away didn't take away my anxiety or grief. It didn't open me immediately to the discovery of myself. It only plunged me deeper into the depth of my pain and fear.

Ultimately, Niebuhr writes, our work is to trust in the void — to trust in that from which all life comes and takes away all we love. Four years after hearing the Niebuhr quote my freshman year in college, I was at Yale Divinity School where Niebuhr had taught. Over the decades since then, my bookshelves have been emptied many times. But this little book of Niebuhr's remains, the binding of my own gray book broken, held together with duct tape. I've starred and underlined Niebuhr's words in red, blue and black ink so many times they're barely discernible beneath all the markings.

The truth of the matter is that I've never really believed in the resurrection. Not about whether Jesus was literally raised in a physical body from the tomb or not. But the truth behind the story — that out of death, out of the void, new life comes. I'd preached about it, counseled parishioners that it is true, celebrated with them when they witnessed signs of surprising new life in what they'd considered a dead-end relationship or job, a rekindled hope that something might be possible when before they were convinced that nothing indeed was. But in my own life, I didn't trust in the possibility of new life.

There are journeys in life we would never choose to take, but we do so anyway, because we know that our lives depend on our taking them. In a tippy little boat, on a tiny lake in downtown Seattle, I learned to sail. I discovered a practice that helped me let go of the life I had and discover a new life I'd never imagined. Along the way, I crashed into waves of grief and despair but did not drown. I was tossed by anxiety but did not die. Instead, I discovered parts of myself I'd never dared to embrace. Eventually, I learned what was on the other side of letting go.

CHAPTER 1

Shore School

Livery Checkout: Identify the parts of the boat

I walk down the creaking dock to the cedar-shingled shack on the south end of the lake. Red bike jacket, gray wool socks pulled up over my black rain pants, helmet tucked under my arm. Two overstuffed yellow panniers swinging at my side. Behind me, the vacant lots on South Lake Union are being transformed into emerald green and glass high-rises. It looks like someone forgot to tear this old place down to make room for the new Seattle rising around it. I walk past boats tied neatly at the dock, white ropes coiled in tight spirals, towards the green door. I open the door, trip over the mantle, and stumble into the office of the Center for Wooden Boats.

I remember another day, forty-five years ago. I grew up in Lynnfield, Massachusetts, an all-white town with one Chinese family, about eleven miles and a world away from Boston. The year before, our family — my parents, sister Nancy, three years younger than me, and I moved across town to our new house — a red Cape in a brand new neighborhood of fifty homes built in a half mile circle on what used to be a farmer's field.

Early September 1967, a warm morning, and my first day of kindergarten. I stood in our front yard by the stone wall, arms straight at my side in my new brown corduroy pants and red plaid shirt trying to smile as Dad took my picture.

Our school bus, the wood paneled station wagon, pulled up at the end of the driveway. I kissed Mom goodbye and ran down, anxious I'd kept them waiting. Halfway down the driveway I tripped, fell, and rolled to the back of the car.

I don't know what happened next. Maybe Mom ran down and lifted me up and brushed me off. Perhaps I jumped up and climbed into the car. Maybe I called out 'I'm fine' when I wasn't at all. All I remember is that I scooted into the back seat next to a boy with a fresh buzz-cut like mine looking as wide-eyed and scared as I felt. I closed my eyes. Tried to pretend that what was happening wasn't really happening — Mom standing at the end of the driveway with my little sister in her arms waving goodbye. I wasn't going away. I wasn't going to school. I wasn't going to cry.

I've spent my career walking with members of my church as they'd navigated their way through the transitions of life. I've sat with them at hospital beds and at kitchen tables. I've taken their hands in mine and offered a prayer in the back pews of an empty sanctuary after Sunday services. I've listened, loved, hoped, and prayed with them and for them as they struggled to find their way through the twists and turns of death and divorce, children born and children leaving home, unease of many kinds. I've tried to offer a careful listening presence and a heart of compassion. Tried to point them towards a next step on the way through their grief, anxiety, and fear to joy and new life.

Sometimes I've been too quick to run to solutions or quick-fix answers. Sometimes I've lost my patience. Sometimes I've gotten lost in my own thoughts and feelings. But despite what I haven't always done as well as I could, I also know I've loved and cared deeply for those who trusted me with their stories. I've hoped and prayed passionately that they'd find their way safely through the storms in their lives.

What I've wanted for them is what I want for myself and struggle to find — a way through to new life. For a while, I've been a good listener to others, but I haven't always done such a good job listening to myself. The last years have been a trial as I struggled with saying goodbye to Dave and yet holding on and refusing to let go. It's taken me a long time to find my way to sailing school.

Dick, a gaunt, gray-haired man in a faded Center for Wooden Boats ball-cap invites me to fill out a nametag and pull a white plastic chair into the circle. There's a couple of dads in Mariner ball-caps with their middle school age sons, and a twenty-something year old guy in the corner with a stubble of beard holding hands with a young woman in a blond ponytail and orange fleece vest. Dick passes out a book with a picture on the cover of a blond kid in a floppy white hat and goofy smile leaning off the side of a yellow sailboat in a white-capped sea. I flip through the chapter titles — *Points of Sail, Knots to Know, Reefing, Reaching, Heaving To*. There's a lot here I know nothing about.

Dick introduces us to Elena, the livery manager. She's a young woman with short cropped brown hair, cute, self-assured. She tells us how she learned to sail.

"It was the summer before my senior year in college and I didn't have a clue what I was going to do after I graduated. And then out on a run along Lake Michigan I ran past the sailing marina at Northwestern University and I saw these sailboats flying across the lake. I knew right then and there I needed to learn to sail and signed up for a four-week class the next day. I didn't take to sailing easily. We sailed these little laser boats and I spent most of the class in the water. I would turn too quickly, the boat would capsize, and I'd spend the next fifteen minutes trying to climb back on board."

"Learning to sail was just what I needed in that time of

transition," she continued. "When I was out sailing I couldn't be anywhere else. It required all this physical and emotional energy. If I wasn't fully present, the boat flipped. At the end of the course I went back to school knowing that no matter what, I wanted to be on a sailboat. I really needed it. I hope sailing will be an adventure in discovery and growth for you too," she said.

I look out the window now spotted with drizzling rain as the boats rock by the dock, the masts appearing to scrape the gray sky and dark clouds darting beneath.

Elena goes on, "Our goal is to teach you to sail confidently on your own." The rain starts to drum steadily on the roof. The "confident" and "alone" parts feel a long way from where I am.

"You must be motivated to attend," she continues.

No problem, I think. Once I got to school, I always liked the order, rhythms, and rituals of the classroom. It's nice to sit here flipping through the books, getting ready for a class. It feels familiar, safe, do-able. I think of all the circles of chairs I've sat in greeting my classmates. Maybe this won't be too bad.

"October is a great month to learn to sail," Elena says, "there's typically lots of wind."

The rain on the roof beats harder. *What am I doing here?*

I introduce myself to Simon, the scrawny brown-haired kid with a wide smile sitting beside me.

"Have you ever sailed before?" I ask.

"Oh yeah," he replies, "I went to camp here last summer to learn."

"Oh, that's great!" I smile, turn away. Pause, turn back.

"What do you actually like about sailing?" I ask.

"Oh it's so cool! I love going fast and I want to learn to race. I dragged my dad here so he could learn too."

I lean forward, nod, smile at his dad.

Thankfully, Simon doesn't ask me any questions about why I'm here. I don't have to explain this crazy dream of sailing a big sailboat in the South Pacific. I don't have to explain this sense of feeling like I need to do something that I don't want to do.

Elena rolls out a little cart and a three-foot-tall model sailboat. As she points out the parts of the boat, she asks us to call out their names.

"The front?"

"The bow!" Simon shouts.

"The back?"

"The stern!" he shouts again.

"The left side?"

"Port!" the kid in the back of the room shouts.

"That's right," Elena explains, "Four short letters. The left side of the boat as you're facing the bow is always port."

"The other side?"

"Starboard?" the blond woman in the orange fleece offers uncertainly.

The words run on.

"Keel." (*A large pointy piece under the boat.*)

"Mainsail." (*Not so hard — the big sail.*)

"Mainsheet." (*What? I'm lost. Why is a rope called a sheet and how does that make the sail move back and forth?*)

"Jib." (*I see now — that's the little sail at the front of the boat which has two ropes attached to it called the "jib sheets."*)

"Mast." (*At least I know that.*)

"Did you know there are no 'ropes' on a boat?" Elena asks. "What on land we call 'ropes' on a boat we call 'lines.'" (*Of course, to add to the confusion!*)

Dick passes out short pieces of white rope and Elena teaches us to tie a knot that involves something about a hole, a rabbit, and a tree.

"The bowline is the most important knot, the sailor's knot," she says. "You need to learn to tie it blindfolded. Take it home and practice tying it behind your back," she encourages.

Dick passes out a little white booklet about learning to sail. I scan the list. I have no idea what most of this means.

"Questions?" she asks.

Simon raises his hand. "What if we learn everything we need to pass a checkout before the classes are complete? Can we get checked out early?"

Early? Is he kidding? I figure it'll take me all eight lessons and those optional ones besides that Elena promised to those of us who "need some extra time to build up your confidence." I wonder if perhaps I'll be the first person not to pass a checkout.

That night I wrote a list of what I needed to do to pass a sailing checkout:

Sailors must complete the following maneuvers single-handed, while maintaining control of the boat and using clear voice commands and proper body motions:

1) *Rig the boat at the dock.*
2) *Sail away from the dock and into Lake Union.*
3) *Execute several short-tacks.*
4) *Execute several controlled jibes.*
5) *Sail on each point of sail with proper sail trim.*
6) *Stop and start the boat using the safety position.*
7) *Stop the boat in irons. Sail off to port or starboard as directed.*
8) *Answer questions regarding rules of the road.*
9) *Complete the man-overboard drill using a personal flotation device (PFD) as the simulated victim.*
10) *Dock the boat under sail.*

I remember when I got home from kindergarten I used to dress up in my cowboy hat and boots, a red cape around my neck that Mom made. I'd go outside, close the screen door behind me, and ring the doorbell.

Mom would come to the door, "Yes?"

"Can Peter come out to play?" I'd ask.

There were reasons why he couldn't — he was taking a nap or having dinner and I was told to come back later. Off I'd go to play with my imaginary friend. Once the neighbor's dog pounced on me. I was so scared I couldn't push him off, could barely breathe with him heavy and hairy on top of me. I learned that day that there are things outside my door that my cowboy hat and cape couldn't protect me from. Grew to believe that it would be better to play indoor games and find my way to the adventure I craved in story books.

Back at the lake, the rain has stopped and sunlight glistens on the wet dock. Wisps of fog rise by the rusted steel shell of the factory in Gas Works Park across the lake. The rest of the class is a blur of things I don't understand about "points of sail" and calculating the direction of the wind. I think I can handle this and I'm looking forward to more classes involving chairs and books and learning the parts of the boat. However, Elena tells us this short class is the end of "Shore School" and the rest of our lessons will be out on the water.

Really? You mean that's it?

CHAPTER 2

Leaving Home

Livery Checkout: Rig the boat at the dock

I'm assigned to go sailing with Dick and the young couple, Chris and Stacy. Chris just bought a thirty-foot sailboat and wants to learn how to sail it. I can't believe he actually bought a boat and doesn't know how to sail. I wonder how he got it to the dock.

Dick slips on a slim red life jacket with silver hooks and hands us faded blue life vests with "Center for Wooden Boats" stenciled on the back. As we follow him down the dock he tells us about the brightly painted red, green, and yellow boats alongside the dock.

"They're great little twenty-foot boats that were built by the Blanchard Boat Company. During the Great Depression they switched from building luxury yachts and sailboats to these open-deck day-sailors for working-class families to rent on Lake Washington."

Dick Wagner, the founder of the Center for Wooden Boats, had bought seven "Blanchard Junior Knockabouts" made between the late 1930's and early 1950's. They look it. Beneath the bright red paint on our boat, named *Richard*, are deep gouges, nicks, and scratches. The tan wood-slat seats on either side look worn and tired, the sails sun-bleached and limp.

The rain has turned to a misty drizzle and the sky is a gray sheet of clouds with a small patch of blue beyond the Space Needle. What we call in Seattle a beautiful day. Thankfully, there's hardly a breeze, scarcely a ripple on the lake.

Dick shows us how to grab hold of the 'shroud'" the wire that runs from the side of the boat to halfway up the mast, step onto the slat seats and down onto the deck. We step aboard, each of us takes a seat. Water sloshes below the boards at our feet. The boat rocks gently, knocking the dock.

"Everything's different out here from what's just a few feet away there on the dock," he tells us. "There are different words as you've learned for 'front and back', 'left and right' and 'ropes'. I have a new name 'captain' and you as well, 'skippers'. On land we know how to get around but on a boat we can't just stand up and walk ahead to where we want to go. The only way to go anywhere is to pay attention to the wind. Instead of looking down at your feet you need to look up and out. You need to look for the signs that tell you which way the wind is blowing."

I look out at the lake, back at the dock. Already I miss the familiar world I've stepped away from.

My parents moved from Lynnfield to Lochmere, New Hampshire ten years ago. Most of my mother's side of the family lives in central New Hampshire not far from Sanbornton, the town which my relatives founded in the mid-18th century, where my mom grew up.

They built a small blue house next to my aunt and uncle's house and across the road from the river that drains Lake Winnisquam over the dam into Silver Lake and from there into another river that eventually connects to the Merrimack River and flows out to sea. On the river, there's a dock that my uncle had put in years before. That old dock was one of my favorite places in the world. I loved sitting there and watching the water go by. Although my dad had a pontoon boat, I never learned to drive it. Sitting there on the dock is what I liked doing most. Sitting and watching the river go by — brown leaves floating past, the river turning to ice, the first buds of spring, and in the summer, blueberries along the bank.

Rigging a boat, Dick explains, first involves checking out the hull and equipment on the boat to make sure they are secure. As Dick points out the gold and silver cotter rings and clevis pins, turnbuckles, cleats, and blocks, I remember how I was taught to pay attention to how I looked and presented myself. Dad taught me that well-dressed men always carried a white handkerchief in their back pockets. He taught me to shine my shoes, down in the basement, with the wood shoe-shining box that his father had made. Mom set out my clothes each morning. Pants and shirt laid over the desk chair, underwear and socks folded on the seat, and shined shoes underneath. One day at the beginning of first grade, I stepped into a pile of dog mess in the grass strip along the curb. The older boys who were walking me to the bus stop showed me how to scrape it off at the edge of the curb, and when that didn't work, to use a stick. But I couldn't be consoled, wanted to go home. I thought how Mom had placed out my clothes with such care each morning. I felt like I did something to hurt, to violate all that love she had put into setting me out for school.

The metal bracings on the boat glisten in the sun. Dick pulls out from under the bulkhead at the front of the boat the "three essentials" — a gray plastic pump, faded red flotation cushion, and a worn gray paddle. It occurs to me that the things I've trusted in, counted on as essential in my life are lost under the bulkhead. I don't know where God is or who God is to me these days. I've felt this call to leave Dave as clearly as I'd felt called to take him as my life-partner, but now I'm not so sure this is a good idea. When we were together, we had a regular morning prayer time when we'd sit side by side and read through a book in the Bible slowly, a few lines a day or through a book on spirituality. Faith was what I practiced each morning as I sat with Dave, but now, what can I count on?

Dick shows us how to raise the sails — to tie a figure-eight knot in the end of the jib sheets, tie the halyard to the head of the sail with a bowline, hoist the sail, cleat off the halyard and coil and hang the halyards. Actually, I have no idea what he's doing. Knots get tied, sails go up, ropes or lines or whatever they are called get looped together. Dick tells us it's all critical for sailing safely and with assurance.

Finding the right words to name who you are and where you are matters. I can't keep track of all the new words I've learned today. It makes me wonder if I'll find the words to name what I need at this time in my life. *What is it I need? Freedom? Power? Presence? Joy? Myself? Do I have what it takes to get me there?* I've been searching for the right words to name my experience and find my way for a long time.

It was 8th Grade, Latin Class. I closed my eyes, leaned back as he walked down the aisle next to my desk. I felt the breeze on my shoulder as he passed. *It doesn't get any better than this,* I thought. I always got to Latin class early to be sitting down waiting for Scott to walk by, to close my eyes and feel the breath of air move beside me as he passed to his seat, to feel something in me melt and wonder what this feeling was.

What was it about him? His thick brown hair, dark eyes, broad shoulders, dark complexion? What was it about his angular chin, the dimple in his right cheek? What was it about everything I saw in him — his confidence, his strength, his self-containment, his silent sullenness, his being at home in his own body? I'd catch myself staring at him across the lunchroom and taking a furtive glance when he walked by me in the hall.

Every class amidst practicing conjunctions and translating Cicero, I wondered. *Am I gay? Is this what 'gay' is?* I wondered too if I was straight. I thought about Debbie across the hall — I liked her, I could feel excited thinking about her too, couldn't I? She had a great laugh, and sometimes we talked together at the end of science class. She smiled at me when she passed in the hall. I liked who I was when I thought of liking her. I felt proud of myself, more grown up, like I imagined Scott might feel. Each day I wanted a little light to go on over my head to tell me, to let me know. *Am I gay? Straight? Who am I?*

All I knew was that I was not like Leonard Matlovich. The first week of 8th grade, I'd come home from school anxious to look at *Time* magazine which arrived every Wednesday. On the cover, I was surprised and fascinated to see a picture of Air Force Sargent Leonard Matlovich, a bold headline beside his picture, *I am a homosexual*. I wondered if this is what "gay" looks like — brown mustache, the slant of his head, the penetrating look in his eyes. Does he "look" gay? I thought so, but why? I'd heard about him and was amazed at his speaking up about being gay, admired and intimidated by his courage. I wondered what would make someone speak up like that and bring on all the death threats and ridicule he'd received? Could that ever be worth it? I sat on the couch to read the cover story when Mom came in, asked if the mail had come. I flopped the magazine cover face down on the coffee table.

Later that day, I'd just come in the door when I saw the magazine flipped over with the cover side up. Mom walked in, saw Matlovich, the headline, furrowed her brow and tore the cover off.

"We don't need shit like that in this house." The white curtains Mom had made fluttered in the breeze.

I knew if Steve, the kid across the street was here, this never would have happened. Steve was three years older than me, blond hair, blue eyes, quarterback and captain on the high school varsity football team, had a serious girlfriend. I knew if I was like Steve, Mom would not have torn the cover off the magazine.

I decided that day I would never be on the cover of *Time* magazine or any magazine for that matter. I'd never let anyone tear my picture off the cover. I'd hide. I'd lie. I'd be a better soldier. I'd always be on time, sit up straight, do my homework. I would be "fine" and more than "fine" — I'd be charming, funny, and self-deprecating as well. I'd like girls. I'd date. I'd get a girlfriend.

Years later Dave and I *were* on the cover of magazines and newspapers. I wonder what parents ripped the covers off and what child was watching and vowed they would never let that happen to them.

Later that spring, I was in the basement helping Mom with the laundry. Between us, the blue laundry basket that I used to climb into as a little child. I'd squat on my knees, grab hold of the soft edges and rock back and forth pretending I was captaining a ship across the gray cement floor.

Mom handed me wet clothes from the washing machine and I tossed them in the dryer. She was crying. I knew it wasn't good. Knew it was a conversation I didn't want to have.

"What, Mom?" Silence.

"What?"

She reached out, put her hand on my arm, "I know I shouldn't have. I know it was wrong. It was just that you left your journal…"

I don't know what else she said, something about it having been left open on the nightstand, as if I wanted someone to read it. What I do know is that I locked myself away, went away as I had learned to do, deep inside myself.

I stepped back. Glared. Silent fury knowing there was no way for me to share what I really felt, the rage, the panic. What did she read?

"You think of hurting yourself?" she asked, "I don't know what to do — you can talk to me whenever…"

"It's just writing Mom, that's all" I interjected, "Just writing.

Just stuff I think about and write. I wouldn't do that, I wouldn't hurt myself."

In fact, I imagined the ending of my life as a comfort, something I had control over in a time when I felt so little in control of anything. It was a comfort to think of ending this struggle I couldn't find my way out of — how to figure myself out and the mystery of who I am.

I wonder now what might have happened if I'd said that what I wrote was true. I was depressed. I wonder what might have happened if I said I wanted someone to talk to about all these feelings I didn't know what to do with. But in the 1970's in suburban Boston the only people I knew who ever had "people to talk to" were the troubled kids who sat in the back rows at school and smoked during recess. Not kids like me.

Mom reached out to hug me, but I wasn't there. I'd gone away so far inside where no one could reach me. But I told her what she needed to hear, that I would let her know if I was feeling desperate, knowing I wouldn't. In my journal that night, I wrote:

> "I wish I could show how I feel but without appearing wrong."

It would be years before I would talk to anyone about my despair.

Dick pushes us off the dock. Fortunately, we don't get far. We all sit on the same side of the boat, knees touching, the boat tipping back slightly to catch any whisper of wind. Nothing's catching. I think of the goofy kid in the floppy white hat on the book cover as we bob up and down going nowhere.

This isn't so bad. I can do this. A faint breeze flutters the sail. We barely make it out of the channel into the lake.

I look back at the glassy skyscrapers that ring the south

shore of the lake and all those orange and yellow construction cranes. I count thirteen today. I wish the city could have stayed like it was, quiet and still like out here on the lake, our boat going nowhere.

I learned how to charm my kindergarten teacher, Mrs. Badger that year in kindergarten. I always followed the rules, raised my hand, spoke when called upon, stood quietly in line, pushed in my chair. At our kindergarten graduation ceremony, I wooed the parents with the song I memorized, hands at my side, rabbit ears on my head,
"Peter Rabbit lost his jacket.
Peter Rabbit lost his shoes.
Peter Rabbit disobeyed his mother.
And for that there's no excuse."

Ever since then, I've counted on my ability to charm my way through challenging circumstances. But as Dick has us take turns moving the tiller back and forth, holding the mainsheet, pulling in and letting out the boom, I realize this sailing business is different. The boat could care less about being charmed. There's a skill to learn that no amount of charm can help me master. I smile at the couple beside me, nevertheless, glad we're going nowhere, just bobbing up and down, catching glances of a gentle breeze.

CHAPTER 3

Be Still and Know

Livery Checkout: Sail away from the dock and
into Lake Union

Its just a few days later and I'm here for my second lesson. The day looks promising — sunny, warm, and scarcely a breeze. A gentle rippling on the lake and a few listless sailboats going nowhere fast. Just my kind of day to sail. I meet my instructor Charles on the dock, a gray-bearded retired tugboat captain from Australia with a blue Fedora cap. His face creased by sun and wind, sparkling blue eyes. He's a short man like me, a compact, solid presence, and something about him, an at-homeness in himself I long for.

Charles cups a mug of coffee in his hands. The steam wafts up over his gray beard like the fog lifting off the lake this early Saturday morning.

"Where's the wind?" he asks. I see the American flag flopping listlessly above the Museum of History and Industry. I hear the faint clinking of ropes against the masts. *There's wind somewhere, but where?* I look around. Then I feel it, a flutter, a cold brush on my right cheek.

"Somewhere over there?" I gesture vaguely towards St. Mark's Cathedral on Capitol Hill.

He shakes his head. I turn like I've seen him do, hand extended like he's preparing to catch a passing ball.

"Over there?" I motion across the lake towards the rusted smokestacks at Gas Works Park. He nods. The wind is coming from the north.

As I step aboard, I repeat the names of the parts of the boat that I remember out loud.

"I'm pulling down the — what is that called again? — of yes, the MAIN HALYARD to raise the MAINSAIL. I am stepping up on the BOW and pulling down the JIB HALYARD to raise the JIB...."

Charles nods as he pushes us off, steps aboard. The boom flips above my head to the other side of the boat, the sails fill. I cower in my seat, hold my breath as we tack our way down the channel, the boom flipping back and forth above our heads. We pass the brightly painted boats moored on the dock — Betsy Jane, Richard, Pamela, Footloose. He points out the white and blue flags on top of the Museum of History and Industry flapping gently in the wind to our left, the bright tricolored flags on the yachts across the channel fluttering the other way.

"No matter what's happening over there with the wind, the only thing that matters is where the wind is right here on this boat," he says. Charles points out the short piece of green yarn, the TELL-TALE, which shows which way the wind is blowing here. The wind is coming from the northwest right now, under the Aurora Bridge. We turn north, head up into the wind.

Once we are out on the lake, Charles asks, "Do you see it? The thin blue line out there, half-way across the lake?" I see the gray water and small rippling waves. I see what a far way we are from shore. I squint where he's pointing in hopes I will see it. I open my eyes wide — I can't see any thin blue line.

A week before this day, I'd stood in front of a Juan Miro painting at a special exhibit in the Seattle Art Museum and laughed out loud in the crowded room. I couldn't see exactly how he did it, but Miro saw what I missed seeing all the time. In blue lines, red dots and yellow squiggles, he'd captured the essence of what at last I saw was a beautiful smiling young woman. It didn't look anything like a real woman of course, and yet it was somehow exactly her. Miro captured not only the basic outline of her form but the depth of who she was — bold, bright, mischievous, full of life. I wandered through the exhibit laughing at Miro's gift at seeing what I so often missed.

This day, out here in the boat, Charles points again at the thin blue line on the lake. "Out there where the water is lighter, just over there. That's where the gust is coming from. It'll be here in a few moments to catch us."

I scan the water, trying to see whatever he sees that's coming towards us. Something creaks above my head. The sails flutter, shake, snap, and fill with wind. Suddenly we are rising up and further up about the waves. I grip the side of the boat. My feet slip on the wet floorboards. I lean back off the side of the boat as far as I dare, trying to drive the boat down on the water. We keep rising higher, higher above the waves.

"Are you sure! Are you sure this is alright?!" someone yells.

After I'd just finished my first year at Yale Divinity School, I found an internship as a Summer Assistant Minister in the United Church of Christ church in a small rural community of stone walls, colonial-era houses, and horse farms just off the rocky coast of Connecticut. It was a still humid day in late June when I climbed into the pulpit, the clear pane windows in the church flung open wide on the town green to catch a breeze that wasn't there. I was surprised and delighted to see Dave and three friends who had driven over from New Haven early that morning to hear me preach my first sermon.

The scripture text was the story in the Gospel of Mark called "The Stilling of the Storm." Jesus has been doing what Jesus does in his disciple Peter's hometown of Capernaum — preaching, teaching, and healing — when he decides that they need to go across to the other side of the Sea of Galilee. Along the way, Jesus falls asleep in the stern of the boat. While he sleeps, a storm comes up that sends their little boat tossing in the wind and the disciples crying out in panic. Fearful that they might drown, Peter shakes Jesus awake, "Teacher! Do you not care if we should perish?"

Jesus wakes and commands the storm to cease. The wind dies down, the sea stills. Jesus reprimands his disciples for their lack of faith.

I don't remember much about the sermon, but I remember that I argued with Jesus. I couldn't understand why Jesus would yell at the disciples for being afraid. I wondered why he wasn't afraid himself; it felt unreal that he wouldn't be.

At the end of the worship service I stood at the door shaking hands. Susan was the last in line, a pious middle-aged woman, her long black hair drawn back in a tight bun. I'd heard her talk a lot about Jesus, praying for the many people on her prayer list, her schedule for reading a passage of the Bible each day. She looked down at me with her dark eyes, pursed lips, a half smile.

She took my hand, patted it, "Someday you'll understand," she said and walked away. I've thought of that encounter many times over the years because the truth is, I still don't understand. I don't know what it means to be calm and trusting in the middle of a storm.

And then I remember a Saturday morning ten years before this second sailing lesson, at a meditation retreat. I'd shown up at 4:30 a.m., left my shoes and socks in the rack at the door as instructed and climbed the wooden stairs to the L-shaped room at the top of the old three-story house. Tall windows looked out on the tops of trees just beginning to bud brilliant green.

Black cushions with black pillows on top were placed around the edges of the white-walled room. I found a spot in front of a tall open window, tried to sit with my legs folded like the man next to me. The small room slowly filled with a dozen people, some with shaved heads, others with long black robes and floppy black bibs around their necks. Incense from the little altar table in the corner with a round bellied Buddha wafted through the room. I looked around and saw how everyone sat with their legs crossed and knees resting on the mats. I sat back on my pillow, then further up, but no matter which way I tried I couldn't get my knees down on the mat like everyone else. *Maybe this too is all right,* I thought, my knees floating several inches off the ground.

A sharp clap of wood. A bell rang several times. I stared at the worn wooden floor as instructed, wondered what it meant to "soften your gaze." I heard the old man with wispy white hair breathing heavily beside me. Birds sang outside, a crow squawked. I felt the cold breeze blowing in the window behind me, wished someone would shut the window. I sat, tried to breathe, to take a deep breath. Couldn't. My chest ached. My shoulders ached. My head itched. It felt like a fly was crawling up my arm. I wondered why I was here. I wanted to go home. This was a crazy idea to come. I went back to trying to just sit here, breathe, and listen as we'd been instructed. Took another breath. And then I felt it. *There was something in my hands.*

Back out on the lake, I grip the side of the boat, lean out, hoping it will drop the boat down onto the surface again. Instead I slide on my seat, my sneakers slipping on the wet deck. The boat continues to tip higher up above the waves.

A voice yelling, "Are you sure? Are you sure this is all right?!"

Two years before that meditation retreat, I knew that something was not all right. I was 39 and felt I needed to "die" to something. Although I had no idea what I meant when I said that, I had a feeling that I was holding onto something or something was holding onto me that I needed to release. I felt that if only I could let go of whatever it was, my forties would blossom in abundant new life.

I asked my spiritual director what I might do. Spiritual Direction, the practice of going to see someone once a month to talk about your life and where the Spirit was moving in and through it, was relatively new among Protestants. I was introduced to it in Chicago and I had grown to like this way of 'talking' prayer with someone.

I was surprised when I moved to Seattle that a colleague recommended I consider seeing Genjo, a Zen Buddhist priest for spiritual direction. I wondered why I should want to see a Buddhist and why I wouldn't go see a Catholic priest as I had in the past.

But there was something about seeing Genjo that felt right even though I had no idea why. Periodically, he talked about Zen things that I didn't understand and wasn't particularly interested in, but he knew his Bible better than I did and was a wise, kind man. I trusted him.

We began our sessions with sitting for a minute in silence. At the end of the minute some New Age flute music would come on. I'd open my eyes. I'd begin to talk. I liked this time the best — the flute music and the beginning of the talking part.

I asked Genjo about this feeling I'd had about needing to die to something. He suggested several ways I might let go and die to what I needed to. He told me about someone he knew who went to the desert and rented a cabin for a week, another who went on a solo hike in the wilderness. He suggested, in passing, that I could also consider a weeklong intensive meditation retreat with his Zen Buddhist community. I knew right away that this was what I needed to do. Although I'd never meditated and didn't like sitting still or being silent, I made a commitment to go.

A year and a half later in late June I cleared my calendar and gathered my courage to go on the weeklong meditation training. To prepare for whatever "dying" I was going to do I'd written what I'd called "Letters of Release" to Dave, my parents, sister, nieces and nephews, my aunts, grandmother, a few friends, my congregation, and even one to God, Jesus, and the Holy Spirit. I didn't have a lot of regrets to share or forgiveness to ask for, but a lot of gratitude and love to express. I stuffed the letters into a file folder next to my will, expecting they'd be distributed after I died. I wasn't sure, but I felt like something in me might die in the coming week.

Someone on the boat cries again, his voice constricted into a high-pitched squeak. "We're going over!"

And suddenly, I am back in that day at the meditation hall. My left hand resting on top of my right there in my lap, thumbs pressed together, the cool breeze from the window behind me on my back. I shivered and I felt it — there was something in my hands. Something I'd never felt before.

I squeezed my eyes tight. Tears streamed down my cheeks and dripped onto my hands. I opened my mouth, tried to take deep breaths, panted instead. My chest ached. Something was so not all right.

At last the little bell rang, one, two, three times. Another clap of wood and I sprang up as soon as the break was announced, cut ahead of Genjo, went straight into the little bathroom across the hall, locked the door and buried my head in the white bath towel.

What was happening? What was happening to me?

Genjo called it a "kensho," a sudden awakening. All I knew was that I couldn't stop crying. All week I sat on the pillow and wept silently, the tears dripping down my face onto my hands. I never knew there could be so many tears, so much wetness and grief. And sometimes, when I wasn't crying, I breathed. Let go and breathed.

I've wondered on this time so much over the years and what it all meant. What I think I know now is that it was the first time or the most powerful time that I'd ever felt what it is to be a self, I mean, myself. What it is to have hands. What it is to have a body, to be a body. How could I have come to be forty-one years old and not realize I was alive in such a visceral way?

Out on the boat, wide-eyed with fear, convinced the boat is going over, I hear Charles say, "We're just fine" and something about a keel under us.

Justin was twenty-one when he went out for a hike in the middle of the night. It was a week before they discovered his body at the bottom of the ravine. Last week the sanctuary was packed with high school and college friends, his family. I looked out, began the memorial service as I always did with the beginning lines of Psalm 46, "God is our refuge and strength, a very present help in trouble. Therefore we will not fear...."

I'd recited so many times those words that conclude with an invitation to "be still and know that I am God." They are a reminder that when there are no words beyond the tears, grief, and rage, to be still and acknowledge it all. All the complicated feelings of grief that we don't know what to do with.

I want to believe, to trust that there really is a keel under us. That even though I can't see it, I want to know it's there. I want to know that I can trust and be still when I'm not feeling still at all. Instead, out on the water today, another gust as we heel up higher and close in on the dock. I grab for the side, close my eyes. *Get me out of here alive,* I pray.

At the end of that first meditation retreat, I stood in the little garden in the front of the house my backpack on, sleeping bag tucked under my arm. Genjo was digging a hole to plant a flowering yellow shrub. The old man with wispy white hair asked, "So, are you coming back?" All week he'd been asking me during breaks, insistent, prying, "Why are you looking so sad? What's there to be sad about?" I didn't know why I'd been so full of tears all week or whether I'd come back, but I did know I'd head home, home with Dave.

At last, the sailing lesson is over. We come up alongside the dock and I step off, bow line in hand. After helping Charles take down the sails, I waver down the dock, the breeze at my back. My next lesson is the following Saturday.

CHAPTER 4

The Winds of Change: Learning to Tack

Livery Checkout: Execute several short tacks

What Should I Do with My Life?
A scribbled note on a scrap of paper
Crumpled on the table at the end of class
A writing assignment, and me with no answer,
"What should I do with my life?"

But then, in he came
Strutting into the room the next day
At the beginning of class,
The famous author from some school back East
Shirt unfurled half way down his chest
Curly black and flowing hair
Circling the table,
Demanding our names
Sordid stories of whisky, women,
Generous thighs and easy sex
The famous authors
With whom he'd stumbled from bars.

I sat appalled, entranced
Wondering how he'd found his way to
Five bestsellers and such bravado.
It wasn't my question,
But here I was lingering at the end of class
Waiting my turn
Desperate to know,
"You see I have this time this spring
And wonder what I should do…"

As the class cleared,
Leaving us alone, he looked at me clear —
All pretense and posturing gone,
"If I were you, I'd live into my dream,
And write my ass off."

And then, he's gone.
An open window,
An empty room,
Squinting back tears
As I wonder where it all might lead
If I follow my dream to the only answer I need —
To live my life.

A beautiful crisp fall morning. I come down for my third sailing lesson and meet Doug, who is seventy-something, has sailed everywhere, and hopes I want to do the same. Everything about him is moving, restless. His hands and his head shake periodically as his eyes drift down, his white beard blowing in the wind. As I've come to expect, he too asks me to find the wind.

I'm standing next to him on the dock beside our boat hands in the air, struggling to determine where it's coming from.

"Is it somewhere over there?" I ask pointing vaguely towards the skyline of the city.

No? But where is it then? Where's the wind?

As he sails the boat out of the channel into the lake, Doug tells me he's going to teach me today about tacking, something about turning the bow of the boat through the wind. But the first thing in sailing that I need to know is where the wind is coming from. That for me is always the tricky part. *There's wind today, but where?*

"Over there?" I try again, gesturing hopefully towards the antennae on the top of Queen Anne.

"That's right, just about there," he responds, pointing a bit further South towards the Space Needle as he brings the boat around facing that way. The sails flap loudly. The boom swings back and forth above our heads. Now I feel it, the wind cold on my face, a few drops of rain. I grab for my ball-cap to keep it from blowing off. The boat rocks. I wonder how long the lesson will last.

On another cool and cloudy October day, thirty years ago, I'd just started my freshman year at Colgate University in upstate New York. It was a strange choice of a school for me. Colgate was well known as a jock and fraternity school and I'd never been a jock and had specifically wanted to avoid colleges with fraternities. But in the summer between my junior and senior years of high school I'd attended a summer school at Colgate for high school students. I'd read *Portrait of an Artist as a Young Man*, *War and Peace*, and *Madame Bovary* lying on my white beach blanket in the grassy field above the campus working on my tan along with my reading. I loved it up there — the long view down the valley, rolling hills spotted with green fields, and white silos, the gold dome of the chapel poking out above the treetops.

Especially, I loved the sky. The vast swath of sky where I'd watch the towering white cumulus clouds move slowly down the valley. I fell in love with that beautiful, quiet, cloudy place where I could watch the wind move through the world around me.

Colgate had long ago sent packing the thirteen Baptists who'd started the college and sent them north to Rochester where they started Colgate Rochester Divinity School. But a remnant of the school's religious roots remained. All freshmen were required to take a semester-long course, "Introduction to Philosophy and Religion." I'd volunteered to do a ten-minute extra-credit report in my class on the conclusion of the Gospel of Mark.

I grew up in a church-going family. We attended Centre Congregational Church, the large white church with a tall steeple on the town common in Lynnfield. Despite attending a lot of church school, I'd never read much of the Bible myself and the ending of the Gospel of Mark was a complete surprise to me.

In Mark's account, three days after Jesus is crucified, three women go to the tomb to anoint Jesus' body with spices. When they arrive, they find that the stone blocking the tomb had been rolled away and an angel is sitting inside where they'd expected to see the body of Jesus. The angel tells the startled women that Jesus has been raised and is not there.

Then, the angel says, "Go tell his disciples and Peter that he is going ahead of you to Galilee where you will see him as he told you." The Gospel concludes with the women fleeing the tomb, "for terror and amazement had seized them; and they said nothing to anyone for they were afraid" (Mark 16:8). What an ending to the story!

I don't remember what I said in my report, but I remember that I thought it had gone well and the guy who lived across the hall in my dorm said I did a great job. I shoved my books in my backpack as I glanced at my watch. I realized I was going to be late for gym class, so I took off running down Heartbreak Hill, past the library and the back of the Student Union, around the garbage bins, across the parking lot and into the gym. Everyone had already gone to class. The locker room was empty. I put my backpack down on the wooden bench beside me.

I looked up at the frosted glass window high above me, the row of tall gray lockers. I crossed my right leg over my left knee to untie my tennis shoes. Then I felt it — this pulsing warmth in the center of my chest that radiated up into my cheeks. I broke into a wide smile. Wave after wave of incredible, overwhelming what — *what was this?* It felt like love, more love, a depth and intensity of being loved, different, more personal than I'd ever felt before.

I put my hand on my white tee shirt in the center of my chest, then both hands on my cheeks. *What was this? What was happening?* I knew — although I didn't even know what it meant to say this — that whatever was happening, it was something of God. I looked up at the light coming through the window above me and wondered if perhaps this was what a call felt like. I wondered if I was being called to be a minister. Was I being called to share this love with others?

I woke the following mornings that week filled with this warm feeling that flowed through me in waves. I wondered if it would ever end. Hoped it would, so I could go back to my life as it had been. Feared it might not. People in my church at home, the liberal United Church of Christ, never talked about experiences like this. Instead this was the kind of experience that the super-religious girl on my summer bike trip a few years ago talked about. She carried her Bible everywhere, talked about Jesus a lot, and wouldn't laugh at our jokes. I feared if I let this feeling take me somewhere that I might end up like her or like the perky, smiley Christians in the Inter-Varsity Christian Fellowship on the Colgate campus. I worried what my friends would think, worried what was happening to me and where it all might lead. Mostly I wanted to understand, to make sense of it all.

At Colgate that spring my freshman year, I took a comparative religion class and found lots of good reasons to help explain away my experience in the gym. I agreed with Freud that it was probably a psychological blip in a scared freshman who wanted direction and to feel special, better than the other kids in my class. I agreed with Marx that I'd experienced most certainly a crutch that had to do with giving into some social norms and control. Whatever it was, I figured it was certainly not to be trusted and too embarrassing to be shared. And besides, I had plans to pursue, goals I'd set.

"This is called irons," Doug yells over the wind. He heads the boat up directly into it. "In order to head in this direction towards the Space Needle we can't get there by directly pointing at it. Instead, we need to tack, to zigzag our way forward about forty-five degrees off the wind."

He points out the tell-tales, flapping strings of green yarn that show the wind's position, and something about the tiller. I nod, feigning comprehension. In fact, nothing's clear. I hold tight to the side of the boat as Doug steers this way and that through the wind. I hope the lesson will soon be over.

Instead, he shows me how to tack. Brings the boat up close to the wind so that it blows just off the side of the bow.

Over the flapping sails shouts, "The captain says, 'Ready about!' The crew responds, 'Ready!'"

"Ready!" I call, uncertain what I'm ready for.

"Then the captain cries, 'Helms a lee!' as I push the tiller or helm across to the leeward side — the side of the boat on the opposite side from where the wind is coming from. I hold it there until the jib sheets flutter to the other side."

I have no idea what he's talking about. All I know is the boat is moving, the heavy white boom is creaking, now knocking across to the other side of the boat as the mainsail ceases its mad fluttering and snaps full of wind, sending the boat rising above the water. I hold my breath, close my eyes, praying again that the hour-long class will soon be over.

Of the many things on my list of things I don't like about sailing, I hate tacking the most. I tense up just thinking about the need to tack and right in the middle of moving through the wind with the furious flapping of sails, I lose courage in all the commotion. Time after time I pull the tiller back instead of pushing it forward to the other side and holding it there. Time after time I pull us back into the direction we are headed instead of onto the new tack where we are supposed to be. Sometimes, and more often than I care to admit, I close my eyes, grab on tight and push across. That's not a very good way to sail.

I've not been a natural tacker in my life either. Instead I've been proud of how relentlessly I've pursued my goals. When others have given up, I've kept on going, straight ahead, fighting the odds, exhausting myself as necessary to keep on keeping on. No forty-five degrees off the wind for me. It's changing direction that's hard.

Knowing how to keep on, I tried to put aside that crazy experience in the gym during my freshman year and kept on at college following my plans. I went to Colgate to study political science. I planned to attend the semester long study program on American Government in Washington, D.C. I intended to learn Spanish, perhaps go to law school and into the Foreign Service.

Unfortunately, my political science classes were not my favorite classes and although I walked around my freshman year with hands full of Spanish flash cards, I couldn't understand a word my Spanish teacher said and answered any of her questions with an enthusiastic 'Si!' I did an internship with a lawyer during January term and after two hours in his office realized that I would hate a job sitting at a desk all day and chasing little kernels of facts found in thick dusty tomes.

I kept on. Kept on pursuing my studies and commitment to the way I'd planned. Kept on and tried to push aside that strange experience in my freshman year that might lead me to change or at least consider the possibility of changing directions.

I figure I come by my resistance to change honestly. My relatives on my mother's side of the family came to Massachusetts Bay Colony in 1634. They later settled in central New Hampshire and founded the town of Sanbornton. Most of my relatives still live close by. On my Dad's side, three Ilgenfritz brothers came over in the 1760's, found home in York, Pennsylvania. Most of their descendants also never left this area. The listings for 'Ilgenfritz' take up three full pages in the York phonebook.

And I've fought change so many times with Dave in the past. I tried to move out, faltered, reeled myself back into the same familiar tack instead of across and into the new. Pulled back when the emotions got loud. Pulled back when it felt like I might actually leave and set out in a new direction. And so I stayed far too long when I needed to move on. It didn't serve Dave nor me. The thing is I wanted our relationship to work. I'd always assumed we'd celebrate our 50th wedding anniversary together. I wanted especially something to work in me that wasn't working anymore. I wanted to understand why I felt called to change course into some kind of further maturity, some kind of selfhood that necessitated a change. I struggled with why I felt called to leave and why I felt like I needed to do this journey in the next season of my life alone.

It took me months to learn that I couldn't tack while tense and with my eyes closed. Instead, I had to learn to keep my eyes open and focused on the point ahead where I was going. Keep my breath quiet, my concentration strong.

"Do you feel it?" Doug asks every time we're out for a lesson, "Do you feel it?"

Feel what? I wonder. *Like I'm a little less afraid?*

Two years after that experience in the gym my freshman year, I finally risked telling someone about it. The winter of my junior year, I took a class with the University Chaplain, Coleman Brown, on Thomas Merton's book *New Seeds of Contemplation*. I dropped in a reference to my freshman year experience in my final paper. When our papers were returned, I quickly scanned through it, anxious to see what Coleman might say or if he'd say anything at all about my experience in the gym. Next to my story he wrote two simple words, "A Gift." That's what it was, a gift. I knew what to do with a gift. I needed to make room to receive it, accept it, and perhaps even delight in it. I needed to learn to tack in order to follow this call to go where I was afraid to go and wanted to go as well.

My parents came to visit in October of my senior year. They asked me to meet them at their room at the Colgate Inn to discuss what I was going to do after graduation. I told them I wanted to go to divinity school. They told me that they thought it sounded like a reasonable idea. Mom said she could see that as an option for me. Dad told me to go to the best school I could. I wanted to go to Union or Yale, but I also really wanted a year off to do something different before heading off to more school.

Dad said, "Go ahead and go now. Don't mess around. If you don't go now it will be harder to come back and do it later."

My attempts at finding something else floundered. I applied for a Watson Fellowship and didn't get it. The woman who interviewed me for the Peace Corps rolled her eyes (another liberal arts major). And so, I headed off to Yale Divinity School.

Initially, I wanted to go to Union Theological Seminary in New York City because the University Church Chaplain, Coleman Brown, had gone there. I also wanted to get down off the pristine hill of Colgate and go someplace urban and gritty.

Someplace more 'real.' But Union was not what I imagined it to be. The school was housed in one building, dark and old, with the student body divided into caucuses — the Gay and Lesbian caucus, the Women's caucus, the Black Student caucus, the Hispanic Student caucus, the Marxist and Liberation Theology caucus. I didn't know where I belonged.

I visited Yale Divinity School on a beautiful, sunny spring day. The campus is modeled after the stately University of Virginia, designed by Thomas Jefferson. Marquand Chapel with its clock tower and shiny gold dome is at the center of the quad. Unlike Union, most students lived on campus and there was daily chapel. It felt familiar, safe, like I could find a home here. I was reluctant to tell Coleman about my decision, but he said I had chosen well, that it was a good choice for me.

That fall, I headed off to Yale Divinity School thinking I wasn't really going to be a parish minister — that still felt far too intimate a role for me. I figured that I'd go to law school afterwards and into the Foreign Service. Some ideas die hard, even ideas that have served their purpose and done their time.

As I practice tacking today, time and time again I don't push far enough through the tack and get stuck in irons with the sails madly flapping and the boat drifting backwards. Once again, Doug back-winds the jib, the bow turns. We move on.

CHAPTER 5

Ducking My Head: Learning to Jibe

Livery Checkout: Execute several controlled jibes

A week later, on my fourth sailing lesson, Doug is teaching me to jibe. In a jibe, the wind moves across the stern or back of the boat from one side to the other. While tacking into the wind is noisy, the sails snapping this way and that as the boat moves a full 90 degrees through the wind, jibing is eerily silent, quick and potentially deadly. Lose track of the wind on your tail and the boom swings suddenly from one side of the boat to the other. The hardware on the mast can break, Doug warns me, and I don't even want to think about what might happen if my head gets in the way. I realize it's why I've seen some sailors wearing helmets.

As when he explained tacking, I don't understand a word Doug says about jibing. I haven't gotten past the point when he talks about the boom flying from one side of the boat to the other. I grip the side, stare at the jib and once it begins to flutter to the other side of the mast, cower with my arms over my head, and wait anxiously for the boom to crash to the other side above me.

It was early January and the first snowfall in New Haven. The quad of the divinity school was covered in a thin layer of wet snow.

I saw him come out the dorm into the courtyard, the guy that had been in my study group at the end of last semester. I crouched behind the brick pillar in the walkway, packed a snowball and struck him in the chest as I ducked behind the pillar.

He looked around confused, spotted me as I squatted down to pack another.

"Hey, what are you doing!" he laughed.

"Throwing snowballs at you!" I responded as I threw another, missed this time.

He moved into the corner of the courtyard ducking against my onslaught of snowballs one after the other.

"Why?" he said, leaning down to make a snowball himself, "You hardly know me!"

I laughed — it was true. He lived across the quad and his friend Tom had invited him to join our New Testament study group. He was a nice guy and smart. A great laugh. Cute too — tall, thin, a long face and blond hair flipped back on his head.

"And you hardly know me either!" I said as I threw another snowball that hit him square on the chest.

By now he had leaned down and was tossing some back at me. Unfortunately he had a better arm and I got smacked in the head.

"Alright truce!" he said walking over but not before I picked up another, threw and missed.

I didn't know what it was about him. There was something about his innocence, his vulnerability. I liked him.

I dropped my snowball, held out my hand. "Peter," I said.

"Dave."

Dave and I became friends, then best friends our second year at divinity school. We met for lunch every Wednesday at the Forestry School dining hall. Dave did things like that, set up regular meeting times for conversations. I was so glad I was included in his circle of friends. I'd never had a friend like Dave. I could talk to him like I'd never talked with anyone else.

I could tell him about the real things that were going on with me, the kind of things I'd told no one about.

One day at lunch, I gathered my courage to tell him about what happened with Ted, my supervisor at my summer job working as an assistant minister at that small church along the rocky Long Island coast.

Ted invited me to go hiking with him in New Hampshire in late August. After dinner and beers at the Country Inn, we climbed the winding stairs to the top floor room — two small single beds under the low eaves. We said goodnight, I turned over and was soon asleep.

In the middle of the night, I heard him rustling in bed.

"Are you awake?" he whispered.

I lay still, barely breathed. I knew I didn't want him to know I was awake.

In the morning I looked over at Ted, his head resting on this hand, his chest covered in gray curly hair, staring at me. I stretched, yawned.

"How did you sleep?" I asked.

He paused. "I barely slept at all. I was up all night thinking about how I want to make love to you."

There are moments where your whole life changes. Something revealed that made me realize there was a reason why I'd been wary of him all summer, why I didn't want him to get too close. I wasn't crazy — I didn't understand what was going on. Now I did.

I scrambled to find something to say. Said I was flattered, but no. In fact, I wanted to scream, "You have a wife! You're married! You're my supervisor! And who do you think I am! Why do you think I'm gay...or interested... or..."

I needed a good man in my life, a good pastor to teach me how to be a pastor myself. I didn't need this. But instead of saying anything, I shut down, went away far inside into that familiar place — shut off, sad, angry, hidden, and alone.

Ted went on to tell me he'd had a crush on me all summer — that he couldn't stop thinking about me and the hard-on he'd had all night. And suddenly all summer — all that extraordinary summer — preaching my first sermon, the lunches with him at the hospital with grilled cheese sandwiches and strawberry ice cream for dessert, his invitations to afternoon swims, the gin and tonics and steak dinners on the porch on Fridays, the attention he paid to me, the care he showered on me — all of it seemed a sham like he'd been doing these things because he had a crush on me, wanted to sleep with me, and not to encourage and support me in becoming a pastor.

I got up and went into the little bathroom, stared wide-eyed at myself in the mirror. I couldn't believe what had just happened. I should have left. Instead, I stayed. I don't know how I got through the breakfast, the hike, the long drive home, the awkward hug he gave me as he dropped me off.

I hadn't realized how upset I was about all of this until I was sharing the story with Dave over lunch that day. He thanked me for my courage in sharing it with him.

That fall, I invited Dave to join me in New Hampshire at my parent's vacation house for Columbus Day weekend. We walked down the riverbank to the dock and turned over the aluminum Grumman canoe.

I steadied the canoe at the dock for Dave to get on, pushed us off. It was a warm Indian summer fall day, the trees just turning red and gold. We paddled down the river, out into the lake and view of the tripling hills. Piper, Belknap, and Gunstock — my favorite mountains to climb, where we picked blueberries every August and where tomorrow, I would take Dave to climb the fire tower and try to see the point on the lake where we were looking up at the mountains today.

We headed home and let the current carry us back down the river, down towards the railroad bridge by our dock. As we drifted along I slapped the water with my paddle to get Dave wet. Dave turned around, "Hey!" a wide smile on his face and slapped the water back at me. Fortunately he didn't know how to splash with a paddle as well, and besides, it's harder in the front. I slapped the water and doused him again. I put my hands on the side of the canoe and rocked it.

"Hey! What are you doing! We could flip!" he yelled.

"Oh no!" I shouted, "That would be terrible!" I pushed hard on the right, leaned overboard and we rolled off into the river. It was cold, colder than I'd expected, but the shock of it today felt good and bracing. I swam under the canoe and popped up my head. "Hey! Get under here!" I yelled, my voice echoing in the metal chamber. Dave surfaced with his long hair flat against the side of his head, eyes sparkling blue.

Later that night, I lit a fire in the woodstove and we lay side by side on the orange braided rug, looking up at the wood beams above our head. This was the best. The best feeling, just lying there. Perhaps I said something like, "This is so nice." But perhaps I just lay there quietly. How happy I was — so utterly, completely happy. Just being here together. I'd never had a friend like Dave. I felt safe with him. The wood crackled in the wood stove. He brought it out in me — this joy, this peace. I lay there and breathed it in.

Sailing with the wind at the stern pushing the boat through the water, is the slowest way to sail. It's like the feel of the canoe coming down the river, paddles resting across the gunnels, letting the current carry you slowly down to the dock. With the wind from behind, everything quiets down. The mainsail, far out over the water, the jib flying out on the opposite side. "Running free", Doug calls it. It feels like we are hardly moving, but as I look to shore, I see that we are moving slowly, ever so slowly being pushed through the water.

Perhaps it had started that fall day at divinity school, when my dorm friends and I came back after our twice a week three mile run and theological conversations about God, the role of the church, what faith means and why it matters. Tom had collapsed on the grass panting, eyes closed. Sean and Dave crept up to him on either side, pulled up his shirt and yelled "pink bellies!" and pounded his stomach with the palm of their hands. It became a ritual after the runs when we got back hot and sweaty, the quick pulling up of shirts, the rapping of hands on flesh. There was something childish about it and something erotic and something that I'd never experienced before with other men. It became the thing I most looked forward to. The thing that happened that we never talked about.

Sometime later Dave and I found ourselves lying together, he heavy on top of me. I don't know when or how it first happened. All I knew was that it felt good, wonderful. A quiet, a closeness. Lying there, breathing together. That winter we went to see "*Maurice*," a movie based on E.M. Forester's novel about a love affair in the 1920's between two prep school young men. I remember thinking that there was something like that kind of British prep school love that we were feeling, had for each other. There was some kind of closeness that wasn't sexual but a deep friendship.

After we got up from lying together, I'd often say, "We haven't done anything wrong," as if to remind myself that what we were doing was okay. It was also new, strange, very different than lying with the woman I'd dated for a few months in college who was smooth, soft, and squishy. Dave was bony, his whiskers rubbed and scratched against my cheeks when he turned his head. We never moved — never let our hands leave our sides. We were still, just lying there for a few minutes breathing. Comforting. Like love, like friendship, like care.

I knew I loved Dave and agonized over it being a 'good' kind of love and worried over the "*not-so-nice-stuff I feel about* him," as I wrote in my journal. I was scared that he might feel the same way.

Towards the end of the spring semester, our second year at divinity school, I wrote him:

> "Someone needs to write a book about love. All the different kinds of love. I know what it's not — it's not general love. It's not erotic love. No, it's deep, maybe that's it. Deep love. That's hard to write about. It looks strange on paper. It's scary love too, I guess — if you really think about it. It bares your soul and leaves you open to getting hurt. Maybe there's a tragedy inherent in deep love. Maybe deep love just makes tragedy all the more inevitable. But you can also spend a lot of time trying to never get hurt. To never taste tragedy. But then you probably never live either. It's the deepest joys that may open you to the deepest pain, yes, but also what makes life worth living."

A few days later, Dave invited me over to the house where he was housesitting. I got nervous about going, about being there alone with him, so at the last minute I invited a friend to come with me. I could tell Dave was disappointed. The next night he invited me again — this time I went alone. We lay together on the couch in the living room, Dave heavy on top of me, when he kissed me. It was strange kissing a man with whiskers and a mouth larger than my own. It was also wondrous, nice. I'd kissed a few girls before — a girl that had asked me to the 10th grade prom, and later a couple of girls in college. But this was different. Could I let myself go there? Could I let myself feel? He stood up, took my hand, led me to the bedroom.

That night I experienced a vulnerability, an aliveness that I'd never known before. We stayed awake all night, touching each other, the wonder of being here together, such intimacy with another man.

"I can't believe this is us," I said time and again as he covered all my considerations with kisses, all I did not understand and all I could not express.

The next morning I had to get up early to preach for a Memorial Day service, and then back to Lynnfield to talk to the women's group at my church the following night. I remember talking to the women at church thinking all the time *you'll never believe what happened last night.* My body awake in a way I'd never felt before. I wrote pages on pages in my journal wondering what it all meant, not able to keep it all in and yet having no one to share it with.

Dave suggested we might call each other once a month. Instead, we wrote several times a week and talked on the phone each week. I loved Dave's letters with his tiny scrawl and I always jumped ahead to the last paragraph when he would say something about how he was feeling about me.

That summer I did my required course in Clinical Pastoral Education (CPE), an intensive training in pastoral care and in mental health, at the New Hampshire State Hospital in Concord. I loved the work and often wondered if it was people there in the hospital or us out here in the world who were really 'crazy.' I risked telling my supervisor about Dave and me. She was supportive and kind, told me that I could certainly be a minister, that my life was my life and not the church's to fuss with. She held out a hope that one day the church, too, would change. Dave was also doing his course in Clinical Pastoral Education in Ohio at a General Hospital and caught mono halfway through. He had to quit the program and was sick the rest of the summer.

All summer I agonized over these feelings for Dave that I couldn't contain, couldn't keep to myself but had to. It was like there was this secret wind at my back that was moving in and through me that I couldn't share. I worried over what was happening, knowing that there was no way it could work for us.

I had not pictures or models for what a relationship like ours might be.

In the week before our third year at divinity school started, Dave drove up to New Hampshire to my parent's vacation house across the road from the river and dock where we had canoed the year before. I heard his car pulling down the dirt driveway, stop, and the car door close. The knock on the door. All summer long I'd been waiting for this time together. *Now that he was here, now what?*

There is something about opening your heart to another that involves a similar vulnerability to letting the wind take you and push the sailboat forward. There is a giving in to and for another that is necessary for love, a quieting of panicking and controlling and to give in to a releasing. And yes, scary and overwhelming as this giving in is, letting yourself be carried. A putting down of willfulness, figuring stuff out, and instead letting yourself be figured out and taken in the unfolding power of this love.

Dave and I had an amazing week in New Hampshire. And then it was time to go back to school for our senior year, anxious that anyone might notice what had changed between us. Could anyone see that wind at our backs that was moving us together? Were we really as good at hiding as we thought we were? We are all propelled by forces and sometimes you are able to see them, to see those silent winds that are moving someone forward — sometimes ambition, greed, lust, sometimes a love that you want to keep a secret.

There is something that happens in a relationship when you need to hide, secret yourself away. There's a charge to a relationship that comes when no-one-knows. And with Dave and me, no one did — or so we believed. The cover-up made the relationship all the more powerful, potent, and real.

Dave lived upstairs with his roommate and I lived downstairs with mine. We got together when a roommate was out and when we made love it was wonderful, natural, and I wondered how anyone could think it strange or wrong.

I remember too the conversation that fall in Dave's dorm room.

"Are you sure Dave? Are you really sure you're gay?" I asked.

I'd fantasized that he really wanted to date a woman in our class who I'd seen him laughing with. I saw the way she looked at him.

"Are you really sure?" I asked again.

He was sure. He'd dated women, had almost gotten engaged twice. He suggested that perhaps I wasn't so sure. I wasn't. I wondered if I wanted to ask Cheryl out. I liked her. I wanted some more experience dating. But I was also sure that I didn't want to find out, didn't want to date. Dave was everything I wanted in a partner — bright, easy to talk to, a great listener. We shared similar interests. I didn't want to lose him. I remember that day, that very afternoon, realizing all of this — realizing I was choosing to not find out more about me. I was making a choice. It was like I swallowed something — gave something up to get something else. I would deny something — finding out more of who I was — but do it to have Dave. I thought it was worth it, most definitely knew it was worth it, wanted it to be worth it. It didn't feel like it was such a big thing to lose. I've struggled all my life with the messiness, the truth of me — all that I don't know what to do with, that isn't cleaned up, tidy and clear — the way I want things to be, the way I believed they *should* be.

It was that night — one of those nights making out in the back of Dave's station wagon. He lay on top of me, my arms wrapped around his back. He rolled over onto his elbow, looked over at me and said, "If we were a straight couple, we'd probably be talking about getting engaged now."

Yes, I thought, perhaps we would, even though it was only months since we'd gotten together. There was something about this relationship that made me know I was in it for life. We'd talked about what commitment and faithfulness meant. We would be monogamous, not date other people. That decision, that conversation, saved my life. I know it.

Over fall break, we went to Quebec City with a couple of women friends from school. One night, Dave and I walked by a basement apartment where two men were sitting having dinner together at a little round table in their kitchen, a bottle of wine, loaf of bread between them. We wondered if that could ever possibly be us. Would we ever have a place to live together, be together, and make a life together? It all felt impossible and no paths we knew to show us how to get there.

Out on the boat, the mainsail out to one side, the jib to the other, the wind is slowly pushing us forward. For the first time since I've been learning to sail, I hear the distant murmur of the traffic on I-5. I hear the gulls fluttering overhead. Everything is so still. Everything so quiet, except for my anxiety which stays on high alert, watching for the flutter of the jib and ready to push the tiller across and avoid an accidental jibe.

Often, I'd rather speed up, rush through, not give into the slow way of being pushed forward by the wind. And yet, today out here in the boat as we are carried along, with the sails out far on each side, wing to wing, I think. *This is the way I want to open my life. This is how I want to open my heart ever wider to trust in the wind behind, to open myself, my life to the sky, light, everything here and all around. I do.*

CHAPTER 6

Raising the Sail

*Livery Checkout: Sail on each point of sail
with proper sail trim*

I think I'm ready to go. Getting ready for my fifth lesson, I've talked my way through everything I'm doing to rig the boat — uncoiling the lines, clipping on the jib, pulling down the halyards, raising the sails. I take one more look around.

I call Elena over anticipating her enthusiastic approval. Instead, she scans the boat, looks up.

"Good job, Peter, except your mainsail isn't raised to the top of the mast."

"But… " I stammer, wanting to protest that I've done everything I was supposed to do.

Instead, I step off and stand beside her on the dock. Sure enough, the sail is flapping several inches below the top of the mast.

Such a little thing — those six inches, such an inconsequential thing. But it all comes down to that gap, those few inches between not quite there and raised to the top. The gap between good and great flapping there in the wind. Standing on the dock looking up at the sail, I feel like everyone else can see it as well. No, I'm not quite there yet.

Whatever the distance between the life I had and the life

I felt like I was called to embrace didn't feel that far apart. Overall, things were good at home with Dave and I kept saying that I was 'fine' and that the gap in my life between what my counselor called my 'present' and my 'potential' didn't matter that much.

"Are you really alright with 'fine'?" a friend asked. "When you say 'fine' I hear 'bullshit.' It's not 'fine' and you know it and you don't want to face what you know."

Perhaps she was right. No, she *was* right. Despite everything in my life that was so fine, I wanted more than fine. I knew how to fit in, go along, get along, but something in me wanted something more.

I remembered a conversation from my third year at divinity school. A requirement for ministerial ordination was taking a psychological exam. I scheduled mine with a therapist on Charles Street in Boston in early January. I walked up the polished wooden stairs to her top floor office, knocked on the door and was welcomed into the bright room by an exuberant tiny woman with dyed blond hair and a flowery dress,

"Come in! Come in! Sit anywhere, anywhere you wish," she said, gesturing me to enter in with her sing-song voice.

I glanced at the long yellow couch, the two cushioned chairs with wooden arms. I wondered which was the right choice. I sat in the middle of the couch, sunk down low in the soft cushions, my feet dangling several inches off the floor. I knew this was probably the wrong choice. Smiled at her across the round glass coffee table with a vase of red and yellow tulips. I wondered how I'd done so far.

In the next hour, there were questions about what I saw in assorted ink blot cards, a role play in which she played an elderly woman and I the pastor. Questions about my family, conversations about why I wanted to go into the ministry and at the end of the hour, feedback.

"There's a catch in your throat, I can hear it when you talk," she said. "It keeps your head and your heart from talking together."

I nodded, smiled, knew it was true.

In my sailing lessons, Doug kept reminding me that most novice sailors pull the sails in too tight. He taught me to find the right sail position by letting the sails out as far as the wind will take them and then pulling the sails in until they stop flapping. It took me a long time to learn this. I run too constrained. I pull the sails in way too tight and never let them out to fill to their full potential. In not wanting to be too much, I become too small. Who would I be, what might I say if I spoke what was in my heart and kept so secreted away?

After my psychological exam, I mustered the courage to find a therapist in New Haven. I wanted to talk about my relationship with Dave. All these feelings were coming up that I didn't know how to talk about. Withholding what was going on in our relationship to our friends was causing me a lot of stress. I worried about how my parents would respond if they knew. Dave was my first sexual dating relationship and I was full of questions, anxiety, and fears about what it all meant about who I was and how it might change my well-crafted plans. Working with the therapist that winter and spring, I began to learn to talk about my feelings.

At the close of our sessions that spring, the therapist suggested that at some point I might find psychoanalysis helpful. She talked about what I might learn from meeting with an analyst for two years, three to four times a week. She thought I'd take to it, that I was bright and could think metaphorically. At the time I thought she was talking about something that might be an interesting activity for me to do at some point. I had no idea until decades later, when I actually went to psychoanalysis, that she was talking about something that I'd later describe to friends as life-saving.

I've thought often about what might have happened if I'd stayed in New Haven, got a job waiting tables at New York Pizzeria and gone to psychoanalysis several days a week. I've wondered what a difference it might have made to learn more about the complexity and fullness of who I was at that young age instead of wrestling my life forth in mid-life. But at twenty-four, I couldn't imagine choosing another way besides the course I had set for myself — to graduate, get a job as pastor. Move on as I was expected to do, as I wanted to do.

In the surprise of a warm spring day, my senior year at divinity school, I took my grandfather's faded plaid picnic blanket to the park next to the school. Set back from Prospect Street was an old abandoned Victorian house, stately columns by the door in front, boarded windows. I loved to come here and ruminate, write, and think, here in the sun. I'd looked in the bathroom mirror that morning and again was surprised by seeing the face that looked back at me. *Whose angry face is this? Whose furrowed brow and stern grimace?*

I didn't have a lot of compassion for myself. I was struggling with figuring out my next steps and frustrated that I couldn't figure out fast enough what to do and what was right to do now. I'd always tried to do things by the 'book' — by family, society, church rules. I was comfortable doing that. To do something other than what my parents wanted for me felt selfish and was certainly something I couldn't express. How could I decide what to do when I couldn't talk to anyone about it except Dave and my therapist? Often I felt so shut down, so hidden away inside myself that I didn't feel anything. I felt like a hollowed-out shell going through the motions but with no one living inside me. Talking with Dave helped open my anger to sadness. And yet, I didn't want to be sad. What can you do with sad?

I loved Dave. I wanted to talk with him, touch him, hold

him tight against me. I couldn't get enough of him, being with him. What could I do without him? And yet I also knew that I needed to take some time to step away from the intensity of this relationship. I needed to step back and ponder what I really wanted. But how could I both need him so badly and also know that I needed some time by myself?

I lay on the grass by the old abandoned house and pondered all of this. All I had were questions. *What happened to the life I used to have?... How can any of this work?... Why would I keep working at this when there is no way both of us can be in ministry and be in this relationship? In lying about this relationship aren't I saying it somehow feels wrong not only to others but perhaps also to me?*

I wanted to be free to give myself to loving Dave and part of me couldn't. I held on to trying to control and fix what I couldn't figure out instead of giving into loving.

I puzzled over scenarios, trying to feel my way into how each choice felt. *I get a church on my own and Dave and I break up.... I get a church near Dave and we continue to see each other secretly....*and, the scenario we never talked about...*We move someplace where no one cares who we are or what we do.*

Lying on my blanket, I scribbled in my notebook, trying to make sense of it all and figuring out what to do next.

> *"I'm still growing, settling into, learning about this relationship. Being me in it. It's easier to see us as friends. I want to relax into this relationship, have fun with it. Can I let myself be loved? Let God love me? Even as I am angry, sad, and confused?"*

Back at my sailing lessons, in the following weeks Doug teaches me to set the sails. On days with little wind, the key is letting the sails loose to catch whatever they can. When the wind is strong or a sudden gust comes up, let out the sails and the boat will lie flat on the water again. Every sailor learns: when in doubt let it out.

"Don't pinch the sails, let them out, Peter," Doug reminds me.

And I keep on pulling them in too tight.

At the end of my senior year of divinity school, I'd completed enough requirements to begin circulating my ministerial profile and find a church position. Dave was circulating his resume materials as well in the Presbyterian Church and we decided to spend the summer together at my parent's vacation house in New Hampshire.

I had a conversation with a church in northern Wisconsin. Their church description spoke of wedding receptions at the town bowling alley, how more and more streets were being paved each year, and how every fall the whole town went in pursuit of the white tail deer. The chair of the search committee asked if I thought I might really be interested in coming, but I couldn't imagine being anywhere that different.

And then, a call about a church in Ithaca, New York that needed an associate pastor. A full-time position and while youth ministry was part of the job description, it was not all that was required. It sounded interesting — especially the part about not having to be a full-time youth minister like many first-time positions required. The senior pastor drove down to meet me at Yale. He was bombastic, friendly. It seemed like a good church — 500 members, at the edge of campus in a college town, with many deans of various departments at Cornell as members. I loved upstate New York. Going back there felt like returning home, my little part of the world of green hills and an open sky.

Dave had talked about us finding churches in the same city but I knew that I needed some time on my own. I'd never had a full-time job before, and I wanted a place to try having my own apartment. Perhaps too, I wanted things to go on as they were supposed to, as I had planned for them to. I wanted to live into my dream of being a pastor unencumbered by the reality of being in a gay relationship. All I knew was that pastors who were out weren't getting jobs. Every gay pastor I knew who had a position was in the closet. I'd heard so many stories of so many who came out and lost their jobs. A seminary professor I admired had questioned whether coming out to a congregation you were serving was ethically sound. His remarks made me question my own choices. Maybe I needed some time to get to know who I was and who I was becoming.

I didn't talk with Dave about any of this — it felt far too painful. I didn't want to lose Dave. I held on. I lied and held on to him. I struggled with sharing what I wanted and needed and all I didn't know and couldn't figure out. Withholding is another form of lying. Lying has terrible consequences for relationships. All summer we hid our relationship from my parents. I lied to Dave about the position I was pursuing in Ithaca and what I wanted in this time in my life. I lied to myself about what I wanted. So, of course Dave was surprised when I told him that I was the top candidate for the position at the church in Ithaca and that I was going to take it.

I flew out to Ithaca and stayed with the Christian Education Director and her husband in their house near the golf course. After an interview with the committee on Saturday I walked out to the golf course at dusk, sat down on the green, head in my hands, and sobbed. *What was I doing? How could I stop doing what I was doing?* But I couldn't. I didn't want this job, I didn't want to be here, I didn't want to be apart from Dave.

The next day the congregation voted me in overwhelmingly. I couldn't get back to New Hampshire fast enough — I wanted the summer to go on and on. The days flew by until suddenly it was several weeks later and time to go. I wrote in my journal:

*"August 13, 1987 — Our last night in New Hampshire
we lay in Jan and Leanne's lawn on blankets watching
the Perseid meteor shower — laughing, drinking rum
and cokes, holding hands. In the dark where no one
can see, make comments or anything — we were free to
be and watch the sky fall."*

In the coming year, Leanne, the pastor of the Sanbornton
United Church of Christ, would be fired when she came out to
her congregation. Their dog shot in their yard by a neighbor.
They'd leave town in a cloud of harassment and fear. So much
for the liberal United Church of Christ. But on that night in the
middle of August, before any of this happened, a meteor shower
— a blaze of lights streaking across the night sky. Early the next
morning, I headed west in my grandfather's black Pinto loaded
with boxes.

Back on the dock, I look up at the sail and wonder what's
preventing me from raising the sail to the top of the mast. Elena
points to the downhaul, the short line attached to the boom
and wrapped around a small cleat on the mast that prevents the
boom from bouncing up and down — and when tied on, keeps
the mast from being raised the whole way. I get on board and
untie it. It's not the first time I'd missed noticing it when I tried
to raise the sail.

"A sail that isn't raised the whole way is a less efficient
sail," Elena reminds me "it can't take advantage of every
inch of the great sail you'll need."

I pull the halyard. Nothing. I pull again. Nothing again.

"When that happens you need to sweat the line," she tells
me and steps on board to show me how.

That fall, Dave found an associate pastor position at a large
Presbyterian Church in western Pennsylvania, about 500 miles

and a world away from Ithaca. While Ithaca was a college community and progressive, the small city he moved to felt like it was still the 1950's. It would be a hard place for Dave to serve and an impossible place for him to come out.

On the other hand, I made good friends in Ithaca, like Joy, who came to the church looking for the part-time assistant pastor, a woman she knew well and trusted. She was hesitant, unsure about talking to me, the new pastor. Joy was my age, long blond hair, strong and forthright, razor thin. She hesitated, questioned aloud whether it would be alright to talk to me about something, wasn't sure how I'd respond. I encouraged her, promised that I wouldn't run to judge or criticize her. Perhaps I knew what she was going to tell me.

She told me that she and her girlfriend had just broken up and she was devastated.

"I understand," I said.

She said, "How could you understand?"

I said again, "I really understand."

Her eyes got big, "No? You too?"

That winter my first year in Ithaca, in the middle of February, days before Valentine's day, I made the call. An impulsive call. A feeling had come over me at the laundromat that evening as I took the clothes out of the wash machine and put them in the dryer, a sense that I needed to make this call that night. I called at 9 pm. What I remember more than anything else, before the screams and yelling, before being told to get home or get to the hospital NOW — before all of that — I remember the silence and the question, "Are you saying what I think you're saying?" I said I was. And the world, my world and my parents', fell apart. Dave drove up that night in the middle of a snowstorm and stayed the next day.

I flew home that Sunday afternoon after church. My parents had insisted on their need to see me. Dave reminded me that they were good people and would come around, it might just take some time. I got on the plane in Syracuse praying that the plane would crash. Instead, I got off the plane in Boston and approached my parents with tears streaming down my face, my arms open wide. "Not here, not now," they said, and scurried ahead of me out to the car.

The conversations went nowhere, the promises asked for were promises I could not make. On the flight home, as I looked out the window and watched the landscape fall away as we soared through the clouds, I felt more alive than I'd ever felt before. I had set out to find my own life.

I was impatient with my parents for the time they took in accepting me. It took a long time — years. I kept hearing from people the reminder that it had taken me a long time to come to terms with what I wanted and my sexuality. Couldn't I give my parents some grace and realize they too would need some time? But I wasn't patient, didn't want to understand, wanted their support right away. How could I find my way forward without it? Could I figure out moving forward into the fullness of the life I wanted with no more hiding, to be like this sail raised to the top of the mast?

Today on the boat, I take hold of one end of the halyard while Elena pulls it back away from the mast. Something gives and the sail flies to the top of the mast.

The week before this sailing lesson, I had gone to a lecture by Amy Cuddy, a professor at the Harvard School of Business, who had become known through her TED Talk, "Your Body Language Shapes Who You Are."

"When animals feel powerful, they literally take up more space," Cuddy said. She showed us pictures of peacocks preening with their bright feathers arcing in the air, a glorious tropical fish puffed out to twice its size, a great brown grizzly raised on its back feet, an elephant with grey floppy ears straight out to the side of her head.

"Olympic Gold Medal winners raise their arms high on the trophy stand. Runners raise their arms when finishing a race, even blind runners. It's something instinctual in us all," she reminded us.

"Put your arms high overhead. No matter what you think about when you hold this pose, lots of good things are happening in the neurons in your brain that will make you feel more assertive, confident, optimistic, willing to take risks, and receive feedback. Practice this and you'll be more likely to get that second interview. Confidence, presence, passion, authenticity, enthusiasm, warmth all lead to feelings of trust. Trust opens doors."

After I came back to Ithaca, I found a men's group, made good friends with some pastors that I risked coming out to. I found a counselor who was kind and supportive. My sister met me in the Berkshires that spring for a weekend of biking and talking. We'd drifted apart in college and it was good to be meeting each other and getting to know each other again. We talked. She wanted to understand, wanted to get to know me — to see how I'd changed, if I'd changed.

I kept going home, dragging Dave with me for holidays with my parents, in the hope that if my parents were able to get mad enough for long enough, they would get over it. I was impatient with the time it took, impatient with their slowness in accepting and loving me.

I went to see my mentor and the Colgate chaplain, Coleman. He paused, nodded as I told him about Dave and me. Told me that for some people homosexuality was a choice, for others not so. I wondered if my loving of Dave was a choice and what difference it would make if I chose to love a man or if it was something innate in who I was. He was supportive, but not overly. Not excited, enthusiastic for me, but cautious. He commented that he might not have given me what I was looking for.

I led a book group at church on John Shelby Spong's new book on homosexuality. I joined the Tompkins County AIDS Network. I came out to my two clergy colleagues.

The senior pastor at the church was excited to preach a sermon on homosexuality and publicized it in the *Ithaca Journal*. He made it sound like it was going to be some kind of groundbreaking sermon. I was curious, hopeful. Instead he started his sermon saying that when he thought of two men having sex together he wanted to throw up, throw up all over the place. I sat across from him, on the other side of the chancel, wide-eyed. Whatever he said after that — trying to win his conservative Deans over to think differently about homosexuality — I never heard. A couple of visitors that I knew had come to church that day to hear some positive news after their son had come out. They left sad and discouraged — didn't even go through the receiving line.

Afterwards, I stormed into his office. "What were you thinking?! You wanted to throw up all over the place?! I can't believe it! And people came especially because they thought they were going to hear something positive and affirming about their sons and daughters!"

He looked confused, hurt, like I missed hearing what he was trying to say. It was then I wondered if I could really trust him to stand by me and help me raise the sail and come out to the church.

Dave and I met every three weeks in little towns between Ithaca and Kittanning — Gas City, Williamsport, and Olean, which became our favorite meeting place. We stayed at the Best Western Motel which offered clergy discounts, had Friday dinners at Pizza Hut, and breakfast every Saturday morning at Perkins. The waitresses and maître de greeted us as if we were old friends.

We took study leaves and vacations together. We lived two separate lives, separate identities. In January 1989, we took a trip to Nicaragua during the Contra War with our New Hampshire friends Jan and Leanne over the objections of several men at my church who implored me not to go as Nicaragua was on the State Department watch list. I tried to explain to them how I considered this all the more reason to go.

A few weeks after we returned from Nicaragua, Dave and I sat at our regular booth at Perkins in Olean. Dave told me he needed to leave his position. He'd been sick more often the last year and a half than he'd ever been before, and it was time to go. He wanted to go to social work school at the University of Chicago as an alternative to ministry as it was impossible to get a position as a Presbyterian pastor who was out and in a relationship. He made it sound like something he wanted to do, that he could serve a church as a lay leader, that it was all going to be fine. He wanted it to be fine, we both did. He gave away almost all of his theology books to a young woman in his congregation who was beginning seminary.

I had a lot of things going well in my life — I had friends, a good community, a good church. I remember sitting one Saturday afternoon that spring in my dark apartment, in the rocking chair in my bedroom, rocking in my uncertainty. *What should I do?* The congregation loved me and although there was a strong conservative bent in the community, I wanted to come out to them — I wanted them to know who I was. I wanted to make a difference, to do justice, to change the church. But I wasn't sure, when the pressure came and people began to leave, if the senior pastor would stand by me. I doubted he would once the protests got loud and the powerful, wealthy people he had cultivated relationships with threatened to leave the church. Did I want to be a sacrificial lamb? But isn't sacrifice for the sake of justice what faith calls us to? I didn't know what to do.

I walked for hours around downtown Ithaca one night searching for something I couldn't name and trying to avoid something I couldn't embrace. I sat on a bench in the Ithaca Commons and wrote in my journal:

> *"God, you strip away my defenses of strength, self-sufficiency, material comfort leaving me in the void. Don't plunge me into life and poverty only relying on you!"*

What I knew was that I loved Dave. I wanted — and feared — moving to Chicago and being with him and yes, I thought, maybe it was time to go. It was a choice and with that choice, as well a loss. I decided — it made sense, was who I wanted to be — to move to Chicago to be with Dave. I understood all of the loss this would mean and it was huge — my first job, first adult friends, and people I could be real with. I had a life here and a good one. And I was sad here, sad as well for not being able to be open about myself, for not being here with Dave. I thought about choosing a relationship over a job. I thought how that made sense, was a good thing to do.

When I told my therapist that I was moving to Chicago with Dave, he looked up, startled. "You can't do that. You'll never learn who you are."

I sat back in my chair.

"Well," he paused, collecting himself, leaned back in his chair, "I guess you can, you could if....".

Thirty years after leaving Ithaca, I saw Tony again. So curious to ask him about the comment I remember him saying.

He sat back. "That doesn't sound like something I'd ever say," he said. "But it does sound like something you might have thought."

All these years later I hear the question he asked or that I was asking myself — What does it mean to know yourself? Do I know myself now? If so, what do I know?

That spring I came out to several people at church. The conversations went well and I wondered if it was because I was leaving. I had trouble hearing their support. I had a good-bye party and didn't invite my therapist Tony to come even though he'd been such a huge support to me. On the last Sunday, my friend Joy and I sat on the steps in the chancel and sang together Fred Small's song "You Can Be Anybody You Want to Be." When we got to the lyric "some women love women some men love men," several members looked down, held their heads in their hands.

I'm still getting used to seeing what the sail looks like when it's full. I still need to step off the boat and look up at the mast and check it out. I'm learning what it feels like to have the sail raised to the top. When it happens, I'm sailing, I'm living, I'm exalting in my life. I'm not hiding what I know but risking truth, sharing my confidence as well as my compassion.

That's what I share with my friend Laurel later that day, after my sailing lesson, outside of United Airlines Departures, at SeaTac Airport, car flashers on in the drizzling rain, trunk flung wide, and the two of us with our arms high in the air overhead. She's off for a job interview in Boston.

"Risk being big, Laurel. Raise your sail. Show them what you know. You got it, you do, every inch of you," I remind her.

Later that week, it's me again. Out here today on a glorious fall day, sail raised to the top of the mast, using every inch of what I've got. I bring the boat up close to the wind and fall off naming the points of sail aloud as I make circle upon circle practicing all the points of sail — letting out the sails, pulling them in. Close haul, close reach, beam reach, run, beam reach, close reach, close haul. Repeat. Circling. Circling.

I am slow to realize that the points of sail actually make a boat go somewhere. But going somewhere is not why I learned to sail. I learned to sail to help me through my fear which I learned required raising the sail and opening my life to exploration, wind and freedom. Raising the sail and circling through all the points of sail is what helped me get there.

CHAPTER 7

Lost and Found

Livery Checkout: Stop and start the boat
using the safety position

Today, for my ninth lesson there is wind, lots of wind. I push off, step on board. Hand on the tiller, mainsheet in hand, I quickly turn, tack and let the south wind push us down into the channel and into the lake. Turning into the wind and away from the wind, watching the green tell-tales fluttering, wondering if the rippling waves ahead mean that something is happening or is going to happen or yes, now happening, as the sails shudder, the boom creaks to the side, and the boat heels high.

It's been like this these past weeks of lessons, a flutter and flurry of sails and learning. Once again today, I grip the side, shoulders tense, bite my lips to keep from shouting, try to remember how to bring the boat down flat on the water and out of the wind.

"Now watch where you're going. Head up. Head Up!" Dick shouts over the flapping of the sails.

"The other way — heading up is heading into the wind," Dick reminds me one more time. I pull the tiller slightly towards me and this time we turn up into the wind, the boat heeling high on the side.

"That's it," he encourages, "Further, further, keep going — now hold it right there." Here with the wind strong off the bow is the last place I want to be.

Let's fall off, let's get out of this, let's call it a day, I want to shout. Dick reminds me to look up, look out to where we're headed instead of down at the waves. I crouch a bit lower to keep my head out of the way of the boom.

With the wind tipping us above the waves, Dick says, "Hold it right there. Release the mainsail, release the jib, let them luff out to the side."

The boom swings far out over the water, rocking the boat back gently as the wind passes on either side of the sails. The boat comes down on the water, slows, glides almost to a stop. Safety position. The right position to catch a breath, change seats.

After I left Ithaca, Dave and I went on vacation to Great Britain, and we moved to Chicago that summer. We found an apartment in Hyde Park where Dave was starting social work school at the University of Chicago the next month. I'd got a job through The Esther Davis Center, a program of the American Baptist Churches of Chicago, that placed folks like me who were high on education and passion and short on practical experience in year-long positions working for non-profits. Our first Sunday we went to the Baptist church in Hyde Park in Chicago where my supervisor introduced us to the congregation as "Peter and his lover Dave."

We were so embarrassed. *Was that us? Really?*

I'd found a placement as the program director for a new community project in Evanston called BE-HIV, Better Existence with HIV. The Evanston Health Department, city drug treatment center, Baptist Church, United Way, and Junior League had the idea of a drop-in center for people living with HIV and AIDS and their families. That fall we opened a confidential site in the basement of the United Methodist Church and every Monday night I met with the group of men and women who were HIV positive and needed a safe place to talk. Laura from Skokie, Roseline from Haiti, Robert, an injection drug user from Chicago, Phil and Jeff, gay men from Evanston.

At Yale Divinity School, I'd first heard about AIDS from our friend Kathryn who worked for the New Haven AIDS clinic and was adamant about promoting HIV and AIDS education on campus. But whatever this disease was that we were reading about in the paper seemed to have nothing to do with Dave and me — it was some strange disease that gay men in New York City and San Francisco were dying from. Something to do with bars and nightclubs and strip joints and a lifestyle that was not me, not Dave and me.

Looking back, I know now that if Dave and I hadn't been the monogamous committed couple we were, I would have been at high risk for contracting AIDS. There was something in me naïve enough, longing enough for closeness, hungry enough to say yes to who knows what that I may well have gotten infected. As I looked around the table at these young men and women just a few years older than me, I thought, *I so could be you.*

I have often thought that the fact I lived through that time in the AIDS crisis and am alive today, is truly a miracle. A grace. A gift. And as Hunt Terrell, my ethics professor at Colgate had challenged us years before, a responsibility as well.

He challenged us often, "What do you do with the gift, the privilege you have received by being able to come to Colgate? You share it. You have a responsibility to use it to make a difference in the world."

BE-HIV grew quickly. With Ryan White Care Act funds, we expanded to case management and counseling services. More and more people kept coming in, the grants kept piling up, the staff expanded quickly. Everything was new, and often overwhelming. Every Tuesday night I watched the TV show, "Rescue 911." In the half-hour episode folks in three high-risk encounters would be rescued — the folks I worked with had no easy rescue. Instead an AIDS diagnosis meant you had two years to live. Week after week I listened to our clients at our support groups talk about the outbreak of yet another opportunistic infection, the rejection of yet another friend or family member. Attended more and more funerals.

In the stress of a rapidly expanding case load and agency, my steep learning curve and the endless grant applications, I started having trouble breathing. I sucked in my breath high up in my chest. My chest ached. I worried about my health, wondered what was going on. Things were challenging at home too. Dave was unhappy at school and missed parish ministry. I worried about him, got lost and consumed in his sadness and unhappiness and tried to do anything to help make it change.

But as was my habit, I ignored what was happening and just kept on going until that day I was sitting in my office and my chest hurt so badly that I called my doctor. The next thing I knew I was hooked up to an EKG. No, not a heart attack but a good case of stress. My doctor suggested breathing lessons and gave me a referral to a clinician I never called.

I don't know why I'm not so good at this, this slowing down and catching my breath. Why is it that I think that if only I do it faster, do it more that this is the way through? What is it I fear about slowing down to pause? Perhaps it's feeling all that I don't want to feel and facing all I don't know how to fix.

I met with Roland, a Catholic priest each week for spiritual direction. He called my anxiety "a tool of the Evil One" which kept me focused on myself and prevented me from looking out and moving forward.

On the boat I struggled with looking out. I couldn't take my eyes off the waves below or the setting of the sails. But to hold safety position you need to look out to the shore and find two markers and hold the bow of the boat in the space between them. And when you are ready, as Dick says we are now, to pull in the sails and set off again.

Ever since I had started at BE-HIV I'd known that my gift and passion for this work was in pulling people together to start this organization but that when it became a bigger institution that it would be time for someone else to come in and run it. Our rapid growth and my anxiety, all pointed to the fact that after three and a half years it was time to go. I will always remember that day when the tall thin young man with the beautiful face and sad expression walked in and I thought, *I can't do this one more time.*

I felt this immense sadness that the people we served at BE-HIV had to come and seek out strangers in a church basement for friendship and support because their own families, friends, and communities were not people they could trust with the news of their health status or places where they could risk being themselves. They knew that if they were honest about their HIV status, they would have been rejected. I remembered the passion I felt in Ithaca to make the church a more inclusive place. I longed for the church to be a place where people could take off their masks and be themselves. I felt called back to local church ministry and to change the church upstairs into the kind of place where the people we served downstairs would be welcome.

After I left my position at BE-HIV, I went for a retreat at Ghost Ranch in New Mexico and Dad joined me for a week of skiing afterwards in Colorado. Things were changing with my parents. This past Christmas we had gone to China with Dave's parents and my parents to visit Dave's older brother, his wife and our eleven-month old niece. Dave's parents had asked about joining us for the trip that fall, and it was Dave's idea to ask my folks to join us too. We were pretty sure they would say no and were stunned when they said yes. Perhaps it was being far from home and from anything that looked anything like home. Perhaps it was the time to get to know Dave's parents and to see me and Dave together. Perhaps it was just time. But our relationship that was so hard for them to accept became easier for them to accept in this very different culture where nothing was familiar.

On our return, we landed at O'Hare Airport in Chicago, but before my folks headed off to catch their plane to Boston, Dad hugged me for the first time I can remember. It was a hesitant, awkward hug from both of us but a hug, nonetheless. Things began to thaw and change with my folks. My parents have continually surprised and shown me that it is never too late to change and that what you don't think can change in relationships, sometimes does. That honesty instead of threatening or destroying a relationship can make it stronger. Their openness to going on this trip made all the difference for us to begin to learn how to relate differently.

When I got back from my time away after leaving BE-HIV, I began to apply for church positions. I was open about being gay and in a relationship. However, as I applied for positions and had phone interviews with a couple of churches, I could see that Dave wanted to be back in local church ministry too. Dave excelled at Social Work school and got the top awards each year and hated being there. Perhaps we could reimagine how to be pastors.

We'd been together for seven years at this point and I asked Dave about what he would think about applying for a position together. Dave was Presbyterian and unlike the official policy of the United Church of Christ, as a Presbyterian he could not be out as a gay man, in a relationship, and serve as a pastor. It is a huge thing to leave a denomination that has been home for you. And so many gay and lesbian pastors at this time were forced to leave their church home if they wanted to serve a church. Dave began the process of switching membership to the United Church of Christ. That spring, we saw a position for a pastor at a small church in Columbus, Ohio where Dave lived before going to Yale and where he had some great friends. It seemed perfect. Perhaps a way was opening.

Out on the boat I was finding my way as well. I was slowly learning about not just looking down but looking out, about gripping a bit less strongly when the boat heeled and closing my eyes less. When I got overwhelmed, I found safety position, caught my breath. Then pulled in the sails and took off again. Stopping and starting I was slowly learning to sail more confidently.

It's now mid-November when I show up at the dock and Dick looks down at our instruction sheet and says, "It looks like today is your checkout day."

What? My checkout? But I'm not ready, not prepared, I want to interject. *Besides there's wind out there today and…*

But instead of saying any of that, I shake hands with a young guy named Mike who is also ready for his checkout today. Dick goes out in the boat with us — Mike at the jib sheets and me at the helm. There's not as much wind as I've feared.

Dick talks us through, offers correction. Asks us to show our tacks and jibes, inquires about our point of sail and whether we are on a close haul or a close reach. "Now a little bit more, let it out, let the sail out," he reminds me. "Good. Right there. Hold it there."

Safety position. We pull the sails in and we're off again.

I dock the boat and Dick pushes us off so that Mike can take a turn at the helm. Dick steps off after Mike docks us. "I'll watch you from here. Make a few tacks and jibes, each of you, then dock the boat."

He pushes us off. I've never been out alone without an instructor. Mike and I tack and jibe, switch positions. This time it's me at the helm, hand on the tiller and directing commands. There's just enough wind and not too much. I bring the boat in, closer, closer to the dock, pull up alongside, step off. I'm good at docking.

"Congratulations," Dick says as he grabs the bow line. "You passed."

"Good job!" Elena says as Dick fills out our official checkout cards and places them in the little file box on the livery shelf. I can't stop smiling.

"I feel prouder than I did graduating high school," I tell her.

We don't get a sticker, a badge, or a special hat. Instead we get a little blue card in a cardboard box in Elena's livery office that says we've passed our checkout and can take a boat out by ourselves. I have so much more to learn. I know I'm barely competent and I forget all the terms and what to do out there all the time. But I passed. I passed! I can't believe it.

I buy a green Center for Wooden Boats ball-cap to mark the day and ask a family visiting from Mexico to take my picture with my livery card in hand. They hand my phone back to me so I can check out the picture — I'm beaming.

I know all my doubts and questions. I know that I can't imagine actually taking a boat out alone — that feels like a long way off. But Dick sees what I can't. He sees that I'm learning, that I'm slowly getting it. Getting enough of it so that I'm ready to practice myself.

After successfully passing my checkout, I visit friends in Portland the next weekend in their downtown apartment and wake early morning with a familiar ache. The sun is not yet up, the sky just beginning to lighten. As I lie here, gray shapes of the city appear bolder and brighter. Dave and I had often made this trip here together. *He should be here, I think. We'd be going out for a morning walk and coffee. We'd be reading through a book together for our morning quiet time. What am I doing here alone in this familiar place and with this familiar missing?*

I get up and go for a run. Take off and wind my way through the empty city streets. I turn this way and that to avoid stopping at the traffic lights. I find my way to the river, run down a path that leads to a narrow dirt trail along the riverbank — my eyes on my feet as I go down, down, down. The path ends. I look up. A sailboat is moored just off shore. It looks like hope, like a sign, like it's going to be okay, like I'm going to be okay. I stop, breathe.

Knowing

Not knowing
how
to get out
of this sad spin
of grief
I run
out
to the river
run
to where
the path
leads
to the water's
edge.

I stand,
still,
for a long time,
watching.

Rippling waves.

At last
look up.
See beyond,
not so far away,
a boat,
the kind I could
handle and sail.

I take it,
as I do most
anything these days,
as a sign,
that what I need
shall be given.

That the path
is going
somewhere
and not
so far away,
a boat
to take me there.

I run —
home again,
dream
that night
of wind.

CHAPTER 8

Stuck in Irons

Livery Checkout: Stop the boat in irons,
sail off to port or starboard as directed

Emptying

The forest is emptying itself
Releasing a brown canopy
Leaving bare stems pointing
To a dark sky.

We do not come easily to such a time
Putting down, letting be
And dying to what has been
So what may be will come in its time
Which is not yet.

We fuss, cling, wail, hold on
To what has been
And is no longer
Spin out in endless what if's —
We had only done it differently
Worked at it more
Been better people
Made better decisions

That it might not have had to come down to this
As if this emptying were our fault somehow
That we could have prevented it all.

No, we are not at peace
Do not want it this way
So aware of who is not here
All that has changed
The deaths and loss we see and bear
The futility of fixing or escaping any of it.

The forest does not suffer as we do.
It did not fail at keeping summer.
The earth rotates,
The axis tilts,
The forest releases into its emptying
That must come before all filling.

Truly, this emptying
Makes room for everything
That yes, will come,
In its good season.

A month after receiving my livery pass at the Center for
Wooden Boats, I'm sitting on a bench early one morning
in the concrete airport breezeway at Fort Meyers International
Airport, waiting for the shuttle van to arrive and take me to
my hotel. A few palm trees sway in the breeze in a spot of blue
sky by the exit ramp from the terminal. It's warm, a warmth I
haven't felt in months. It feels like a foreign country, a very far
country from the cold, rainy Seattle I left the previous night.

The first week of December, every year for the past ten
years, I'd gone on a weeklong Zen meditation retreat on the
shore of Puget Sound. The "rohatsu" is the most rigorous of the

four week-long intensive periods of meditation practice held each year. The hours get longer and longer — up earlier, to bed later, long sets of sitting meditation hour after hour listening to the surf and wind, the cries of gulls and eagles, the beating rain. It's cold, dark and exhausting. I've loved it all including the drizzling rain and bracing cold when we'd walk outside for walking meditation or "kinhin." It's the kind of damp that seeps into my bones, the kind of cold when it feels impossible to get warm. The week of silence, ritual, rhythm, and rigor clears me out, empties and grounds me as nothing else has.

But this year, I've wanted a different kind of week. I didn't want cold and drizzle; I wanted warmth and sun. I didn't want to sit by the water's edge; I wanted to get out on the water and into the wind and waves. So instead of going to sit with my friends by the shore of Puget Sound, I'd gone alone to Florida to sailing school on the Gulf of Mexico.

Ever since I'd heard about a sailing trip in the Caribbean that a friend was going on during this rohatsu week, I'd thought of doing that myself. However, my web search on "sailing" revealed a lot of high-end cruises and party boats. But as I continued my search, I realized that I didn't want to sit on a boat, I wanted to be sailing a boat. I wanted to continue practicing what I'd learned the last few months at the Center for Wooden Boats. I'd learned the basics of sailing — how to launch and dock, some simple knots, how to trim the sails, tack and jibe. But I still couldn't figure out how to actually get the boat to go anywhere except around and around in circles. I wanted to learn how to sail somewhere. So I narrowed my internet search to 'learn to sail' and began finding something closer to what I was looking for.

I found a course here at Fort Meyers Beach and when I saw that they taught sailing on 'Colgate 26's,' I took it as a sign. Like going to Colgate, I felt intimidated by boats a full six feet longer than I'd sailed. It felt like a whole new challenge. I signed up. When two thick textbooks arrived the next week, I knew I'd found the kind of experience I was looking for. As I skimmed through the books, I knew that I wanted to learn all this — all about wind and navigation, cleats, and the curvature of the sail.

My week-long meditation retreats typically began the day before the actual retreat started. Something often happened on that day that cracked me open in anger, fear, or anxiety. It opened up a question, a feeling that I'd wrestle with all week as my own personal koan. It was like that this time too.

Yesterday, before I landed here in Florida, my landlord offered to drive me to the airport. I'd been living in a rented room in her house for the past months. She'd listened to me with care over a shared meal or game of Scrabble as I talked about my ups and downs of finding my way alone — missing what had been and wondering where it all was going.

On the way to the airport, coming up over First Hill, the hospital towers around us, the view of the Seattle skyline in front, I told her about being on vacation with Dave several years ago in Scotland. We were staying with friends near St. Andrews and Dave and our friends had gone out for a beer. I'd stayed behind, and for some reason, checked my email that evening. Something I rarely, if ever, had done on vacation. There was a message about a Guatemalan refugee who was turning eighteen, losing his foster home placement and needing a place to stay as he completed his asylum process.

Dave and I had never received an email like this before. We'd talked about kids but didn't know how we would balance kids with two demanding ministry positions and other calls on our lives and time. But this opportunity seemed to be just the kind of fit we were looking for — a kid who was old enough to be somewhat independent. When Dave got back, I showed him the email. We both agreed this was something we would like to do so we wrote off a quick note and anxiously awaited a response.

My landlord looked over at me. "I've been meaning to ask, and I know this is really about me and my unprocessed stuff, but are you sure? Are you really sure you want to leave this relationship? I mean, I hear about that kind of connecting and understanding on a big decision like that. That's amazing. Do you really want to give that up?"

"I knew I needed to grow, and I left my marriage with a man that I really liked in order to do something that I felt I needed to do to discover myself. Five years later I wanted to be married again. I wanted to go back. But by then he'd moved on to a new relationship, a new marriage. I see him now once a month. He's my best friend. Maybe it's just me, but are you really sure you want to do this?"

When I got to my gate at SeaTac, I crumpled down against a wall. My psychoanalyst, Carter, tells me I can call him when I need to but because I don't want to be one of those people who are always calling for help, always needy or depressed I never call. *I'm fine*, I tell myself. And then, no. *Not so fine*.

I tossed my phone around in my hands. At last, I called. I usually didn't remember what he said, sometimes just a word or two, a phrase, a tone of voice. But yesterday, I clung to his words. He reminded me what issues were my landlord's and which were mine. Reminded me one more time I don't need to live another's life or way and that I can step out and live my own life, my own truth, have my own new beginning. I got on the plane and soon fell asleep, woke as we descended into Charlotte to change planes for Fort Meyers.

A boat in 'irons' is a boat headed directly into the wind — a boat in the no-go zone where unless you pivot 45 degrees off to the left or right the boat is going nowhere. Getting into irons has never been trouble for me in learning to sail. I get into it all the time. It's getting out of irons that I struggle with. No matter what I do to pump the rudder back and forth, rock the boat, pull on the sails, often I'd just sit here, stuck like I am sitting here today wondering why I'm waiting in Florida for a van that seems a long time coming.

If there was ever a time in my life when I knew something was going to happen and why it was happening it was this church position in Columbus, Ohio. I knew this is where Dave and I would be going — it was where Dave's best friends lived, a city he loved — it was perfect.

The search committee met with us and heard us preach. They were excited and nervous to bring us as their final candidates. They were clear that their church needed to change and meet the needs of their changing neighborhood or die. As they were right on the edge of the gay neighborhood in Columbus, they thought we'd be a perfect choice. A tall elderly man on the committee said to us, hesitant, like he was seeing something he didn't want to see, "I hope it'll go okay."

On that Saturday morning in mid-February, the search committee hosted a breakfast for church members to get to know us. Four members showed up. Two elderly women sat across the table from us.

"Any questions?" the search committee chair asked.

"What's your HIV status?" one of the women asked.

I paused, wanted to say how inappropriate such a question was but instead launched into an explanation of HIV and AIDS and some of the assumptions people had about the disease.

The other woman followed up. "The men that we have called to our church have stayed a long time. How long would you stay?"

"They're not men," the woman beside her said.

Everyone heard it. No one said a thing. Not the folks on the search committee. Neither of us.

We just sat there, said nothing. I believed — I so believed

STUCK IN IRONS • 87

that it was destined that we were going to get this job. I was
so convinced.

"What do you do?" the other woman asked.

"What do you mean?" I said.

"Have you ever served a church before?"

Dave and I looked at the search committee chair and I
asked, "You did send out our resumes and the materials we'd
discussed, didn't you?"

The chair looked a bit sheepish and replied, "We were going
to. But the secretary said it would cost too much in postage."

"So what does the congregation know about us?"
I asked.

The search committee chair said they'd sent out the letter
they'd asked me to write about how I'd come out to a few
people at the church I served in Ithaca before I left. The two
church members smiled at each other watching Dave and I
look crestfallen at the members of the search committee.

The next day we stood at the door to greet members of the
tiny congregation who were coming to church. Many didn't
even pause to shake our hands. The church filled. There were
a lot more people here than usual, the search committee
chair said. Dave led the children's sermon — no children
came forward to the chancel steps at the front of the church.
A few of Dave's friends filled in so that he could complete
his lesson with someone sitting there. Behind us, at the front
of the chancel a stained-glass window of a sweet white Jesus
kneeling — eyes raised to heaven, hands clasped.

After the worship service, the congregation went
downstairs for the vote on whether to call us as their pastors.
I still believed, I had to believe this was going to happen.
I'd asked all our friends to pray for us — I knew that prayer
could, would change things. Despite all that had happened, I
knew we'd get the position. We had to. We waited in the small
lounge next to the stairs to the basement. Dave's dad watched

the proceedings at the top of the stairs. The meeting went on and on. The vote on calling us as pastors came up quickly. A raise of hands — we got 40% of the vote. As they went on about other topics for the meeting — voting on church officers and the annual budget, Dave wanted to leave. We waited. It took someone from the search committee a half hour to come up and tell us we'd been rejected.

I was numb. Dave was furious. The party, the celebration, the things that were supposed to be happening were not happening. The elderly man on the search committee turned to us as we left, "Stay in touch."

Stay in touch? Why? Why would we 'stay in touch?'

We cried on the drive back to Chicago. The next morning I stepped into the shower weeping. Dave was weeping in the other room. Everything was weeping. We didn't go to church the next Sunday or the Sunday after that. Something of my childhood belief in a God who made all things turn out right died on that day. I'd believed if only somehow, we'd prayed enough, long enough, worked hard enough, were committed enough, something, anything could happen. It didn't.

A door closed and with it my faith. Where now was God? Who was this God who didn't answer prayers? I wrote in my journal that night:

"They say we are good preachers. They say we have a gift but the church doesn't want to hear our voice."

We each wrote a letter to the search committee about how they let us down by not sending out our materials so the congregation could at least get to know us, and by making us believe that their church might actually be open to calling us. They wrote back, "How dare you be angry at us? We were your allies." They brought us in with a hope that their church must change or die. It seemed that day the church chose death. So did we.

At the hotel in Florida I'm upgraded to a large room on the top floor with a living room and kitchen, a bedroom with a king size bed, a Jacuzzi in the bath and a sweeping view down the beach and across the Gulf. I look around — so beautiful, so light, warm, and amazing.

Mom and Dad should be here, I think. *I should have invited them when I went home for Thanksgiving last week. There's plenty of room here and Dad had looked so tired. We both could have taken sailing lessons. What was I thinking? I was just being selfish, doing all of this for myself. What am I doing? They'd loved their time down here last winter — they would have loved being here now. And why isn't Dave here? We'd stayed in so many hotel rooms but few as nice as this.*

I slide down the wall onto the floor, lean back, my head in my hands. What will it take for all the voices to quiet?

I remembered a couple of weeks ago I'd been practicing with Doug getting out of the channel when I didn't have enough momentum to tack through the wind. I pulled hard, harder on the mainsheet. The boat drifted into irons, the wind flapping the sails furiously. The boat started drifting backwards.

One of the things that amazes me about the Center for Wooden Boats is that no one yells. When I am overwhelmed — stuck in irons one more time and unable to get out of it, the boat drifting closer and closer to the million-dollar yacht behind me, I expect to hear someone yelling, a bullhorn blasting, a rescue boat flying, someone cursing me out — "What the hell are you doing! Are you crazy?" I expect someone to remind me what a lousy sailor I am and how foolish they are to let me out on their beautiful wooden boats.

One day I asked Elena, the livery manager, why she

doesn't yell when she sees an accident or anticipates one about to happen.

"When you yell, people don't pay attention anyway," Elena told me. "It's just not useful. Never. When you yell it all sounds like blah-blah-blah-blah, like the snapping of the sails when you are caught in irons. I've learned to wait instead — to wait on the dock for the crash or for them to figure out what to do. Sometimes that's really hard."

"But what about when someone has made a mistake, messed up?" I ask. "Shouldn't you reprimand them?"

"When you've made a mistake, that's when you can really learn something," she responds. "Mistakes can be true gold if you really get into them and can see your way out of them. Use your mistakes to learn. It's the best way to learn to sail."

I so wanted Dave to yell. To scream at me and tell me how I'd ruined his life, destroyed what was ours, devastated his family. If only he'd yell, I thought I could forgive myself at last, release the ballast of guilt and shame I'd carried around for leaving him. But all I heard was the silence. No one was yelling. There was only this terrible screaming at myself echoing in my head. *What a klutz! What are you doing! You don't know how to do this! Get out of the boat and let me take over!*

I knew it was grief. Just grief. And I hated it. Whatever I did — drink a beer, gorge on too many sweets and ice cream, run, bike, sail it away, it kept coming back, surprising me around the turn when I thought I'd outmaneuvered it.

It'd been hard to have good days, good times, when I felt bad so much of the time, weighed down by missing Dave and the ache of what happened. Guilt ballast. Sad ballast. Such a familiar weight.

The sails flapping furiously. I backwind the jib to port — nothing. To starboard — nothing's catching. I keep drifting back towards the million- dollar yacht. How do I get out of irons?

"Do whatever you need to do. Go away as far as you need to go to find your way to a new life," my creative writing teacher, Kim, wrote.

Where could I go far enough away that the guilt and shame would quiet? Would I find it here in Florida?

That day on the boat as we drifted backwards towards the million-dollar yacht, stuck in irons and with no way to get out, Dick stood up, pulled the jib sail out far over the side. The wind caught, we turned, took off. Sometimes it takes a second set of hands to get out of the no-go zone.

It's like that today in Florida, sitting again against the wall, unable to silence all the flapping of grief and guilt, at a loss to find my way back to the longing and discovery that called me down here so far from home.

I call Carter again, hear myself asking, "Who do I want to be down here? Will I be the guy who is depressed all week? Why did I take all this joy I'd felt away from me? Is it alright to have it?" He reminds me again that it's okay for me to choose happiness and step out into wonder. I head out for breakfast.

I walk down the beach and find a diner in the small downtown. The restaurant is packed and I'm seated at a table beside a retired couple. They've wintered down here for years, love the warmth and sun, so far from Minnesota winters. They recommend the lemon pancakes with strawberries. I tell them I'm here for sailing school. They don't ask a lot of questions. I don't have to explain why I'm here alone or why I'm learning to sail.

After breakfast I go to find a bike shop where I can rent a bike for the week. I'm biking back when the couple drives by and calls out the window, "There's a twenty-foot boa constrictor at the Farmer's Market. Check it out!" Checking out a boa constrictor is the last thing I want to do that morning. I've always been scared of snakes. But something in me says that I need to go and check out the snake.

I walk over to the Farmer's Market and sure enough there between the stands of jellies, pottery, and macramé sweaters is a small cage and a sign from the local humane society — *$5 to Hold the Snake.* I join the four year old boy to stand and stare, hands in our pockets, at the great snake on the ground with the twitching tongue. Snap a few pictures from a safe distance.

Walk away. I don't want to be stuck in irons. I want to learn to tack to joy. I want to find my way forward through my fear. I come back.

"How do you hold a boa constrictor?" I ask.

"Become a tree," the old man says as he holds out his arms to the side, his back straight and still. "Trees are their natural habitat."

Why is it that I sometimes can't be content to just sit by the pool, to do common everyday things? Why is it that I must sometimes do the very thing I do not want to do, that won't let me go until I do? But 'almost' and 'thought about' do not make a story and I am here to tell one.

And having no way out but through, I stand, arms outstretched, silent and straight, eyes shut, holding my breath as he places the snake around my neck. I break out laughing, trembling with delight. Maybe I don't need to be so afraid.

I get caught in irons all the time, the wind whipping the sails, the boat drifting backwards. I am overwhelmed and scared. And sometimes, remember, oh yes, backwind the jib. Sometimes remember to hold the sail out on the opposite side from which I want to go. And sometimes the boat turns and I feel this immense relief, this being free and moving forward and I begin to breathe again. I'm still better at getting stuck but I'm learning how to get out of it slowly.

My class starts the next morning.

CHAPTER 9

Going Somewhere

*Livery Checkout: Answer questions regarding
rules of the road*

Monday morning, the day of our first sailing class in
Florida. I wake early and take a long run down the
beach. I come back to shave, shower, and find my breakfast
coupon and way to the restaurant on the top floor. The wide
windows look out over the Gulf. What a beautiful place to be,
I think. I see a young woman sitting alone and ask if I can join
her. I can't believe I'm doing this. Who am I becoming!

After breakfast I find room 687, a small windowless room,
with two rows of desks and a pitcher of water on each set of
tables. I introduce myself to Bob and Judy, a 60-something-
year-old couple who'd been dating for three years. She knows
something about sailing. He's here to learn. It will only be the
three of us in the class this week.

Our instructor, Joelle, is about my age with short brown
hair, a hard-chiseled expression and serious frown. She has her
captain's license from the U.S. and Great Britain where she told us
the licensure is much harder. She's sailed all the great places in the
world — Hawaii, the Caribbean, Mediterranean, and South Seas.

"In a world that is mostly water, why not learn to sail?" she
asks. After her mother died a couple of years ago, she'd had the

freedom to figure out where she wanted to make home port. She tells me she thought about Seattle seriously but couldn't take the cold and rain. She reminds me I live in one of the great sailing locations in the world.

Really? How did I not know that? Maybe I live right where I need to be now.

Joelle tells us that to get out of the channel here with lots of boat traffic we have to be clear on the rules of the road. She explains that the rules of the road in sailing are based on figuring out if your vessel is the stand-on or give-way vessel.

"The stand-on vessel has the right of way and must maintain course and speed. You are the stand-on vessel if you are being overtaken by another boat. In other words, don't make any quick changes to where you are heading. The boat overtaking you has to make early and obvious changes to avoid a collision with you. It's key to know who you are in your vessel and what your responsibilities are."

She goes through the list of rules, goes over them again. I always forget, is it port tack or starboard tack that is the stand-on vessel? It's these rules I need to learn in order to go somewhere. Joelle says the key is repetition.

"It helps in sailing as in most things that are new," Joelle reminds us, "to do things over and over again."

All week she has us go over again and again the parts of the boat, points of sail, and rules of the road.

Last week I'd gone to the Van Gogh exhibit at the Philips Museum in Washington D.C. Van Gogh painted the same scenes of barns, houses, fields, cathedrals over and over again. It was through returning to these same places and painting them at different times of day and different kinds of weather that he sought to capture the essence of a place.

I'm reminded of Zen, the practice of doing the same routines over and over and once again over again. Over time, all the fuss about how you are pouring tea or sweeping the floor quiets down in the steady repetition of just doing what you are doing. All there is, is pouring, sweeping, the essence of the action itself. I realize it holds for sailing as well — in performing the same routines, we'll master an art. In the practice of constantly paying attention to what we're doing, we'll learn to see in new ways.

"You can't rest on your laurels," Joelle challenges us. "You must always pay attention and think. The moment you stop thinking, stop paying attention, is the moment that things can happen."

I think about sailing with my instructors Dick, Charles and Doug who seem to have mastered this way of paying attention and seeing and hearing.

That afternoon we head down to the boat. It is strange to be heading down to go sailing dressed in my tee shirt, shorts, and sandals. In Seattle, sailing has been a cold-weather sport with wool hat, gloves, and a warm parka. *Maybe being dressed like this in warm weather is why people like to go sailing,* I think.

We step aboard our Colgate 26 and follow the line of buoys out into the Gulf. Joelle points out the green and red markers that we need to wind our way through as we go out. *What? Where?* Green to the right, red to the left, as Joelle reminds us along with other rules of the road.

"The boat coming at us — who has the right of way?" she asks. She points out why we have to maintain our course, no quick surprises. "Follow the rules and you'll be kept safe," she reminds us.

I think of my own core 'rules' that I've broken this past year. Rules like marriage is forever. Rules like if only you keep at it, everything will turn out okay. The rule that my role is to give others what they want and keep things the same and safe. The rule that the way to make things work out is to give up things myself, even my own happiness. I realize I haven't forgiven myself for the rules I've broken.

The boat lurches in the waves, I clutch the side. The rules kept me safe — and from being all I wanted to be. I need some different rules.

After our rejection at the church in Columbus, Dave and I slowly healed. And then, a turning. Weary of tears and anger, I woke one morning knowing that our call was to keep knocking at the door of the church and call it to be a place of welcome for all. It didn't matter whether we got a job as pastors or not, it wasn't about that. We needed to just keep on applying and calling on the church to look at its prejudices and become a more open community. So we sent our resumes out and applied to any church that listed themselves as "open," "liberal," or was located in a college town or community.

Some friends wished us luck. Our more honest friends told us we were fifty years too early. Yet another friend, a psychologist, said she didn't think couples working together was a good idea. A pastor friend asked why I was trying to get a job with Dave. He knew on my own I could get hired, but as a couple? That seemed a far stretch.

We got rejected from churches we never remembered applying to. Some letters confessed that we'd brought their search processes to a full stop as their committees had to pause and examine how 'open' they really were. Every week more rejection letters, over a hundred in all, that I stuffed in the orange file cabinet in the kitchen. One day Dave said it was sick that we were saving all these letters and threw the pile out.

That fall we went on a trip to the Blue Ridge Mountains and rented a cabin. Dave said we should stop our search — that we should make home in Chicago and find our life here. We came back from vacation, committed to ending our search. Waiting for us instead were letters from three search committees who wanted to learn more about us — a gay congregation in Michigan, a church in California, and University Congregational in Seattle, a large urban congregation that was seeking an associate pastor.

University Congregational was the last place we thought would be interested in us. We had told ourselves the story that some church that was desperate — that had been looking for a pastor for ten or more years in some rural, isolated location might be interested. We'd even talked to the United Church of Canada, the only other Christian denomination besides the United Church of Christ, open to gays and lesbians applying as pastors. We got a letter from the provincial office in Toronto that said, "people think we're liberal but we're actually not," and a phone call early one morning from the provincial minister of Newfoundland and Labrador. He said that he was intrigued by our resumes and would be interested in finding us a placement, but he was retiring and his successor would not be supportive. He wished us luck.

We talked to the chair of the search committee at University Congregational Church in Seattle and then heard nothing more. Again, it seemed unlikely that we would be going anywhere. And then that December we heard back and had a phone interview with the Seattle search committee, and in February heard that we were one of their top three candidates. We arranged to fly out to Seattle in April.

I'd been to Seattle six years earlier with my parents and my sister on a family vacation to climb Mount Rainier. I had just come out to my family that February and this trip was another of my attempts to show them that I was still the same person and that even though I was gay it didn't mean that I wasn't also a tough, strong man as well. Climbing Rainier was Dad's idea; he was the serious hiker, not me. We stood at Paradise Lodge looking up at the huge mountain looming before us. *Wow, was it big. A whole lot different than our New England mountains.*

At the training session the next day, we practiced doing self-arrests with our pickaxes so we wouldn't slide into a crevasse. I threw myself on the ground time after time, knees to my chest, feet splayed wide, the axe driven deep into the snowpack, praying that whatever I did would actually hold.

The next morning we were off, and after a sleepless night at the basecamp, were up at midnight to take off again. We summited early the next morning. We sat in the snow, exhausted, while others had gone to walk around to the other side of the rim which was actually the highest spot on the peak. This spot here was good enough for us. We'd done it. On the way down I was roped between two tall men. I raced down trying to match their long strides. I looked over at the massive cracks in the ice and snow which we couldn't see in the dark when we'd ascended, only told just to keep left. I thought, *If I die on this mountain, I'll be really upset. This is not my idea of what I want to do.*

After the climb we visited a friend of mine from Colgate who lived in Seattle. He told me that if Dave and I would ever find a church that it would be out here. I said, "I'd never live out here. I don't like Seattle. And besides, who would live out here so far from civilization?"

Dave and I got picked up by a member of the search committee and met with the rest of the group at a small noisy restaurant. A young member of the committee was upset and told us that Kurt Cobain had taken his life that day. Later that night I asked Dave, "Who's Kurt Cobain?"

It was a good committee, a diverse group of leaders in the church. A very different feel from our experience in Columbus.

As part of the process to get to know us, the committee had arranged to listen to us preach at a church north of Seattle. We left early Sunday morning and stopped to see fields of bright tulips on the way. I preached for the first service, Dave for the second. It was a long, intense weekend of lots of meetings, conversations, and a good introduction to what life would be like if we were called to serve here.

Out in the Gulf in Florida, we put the sails up. A blue sky, gentle warm breeze. Joelle says we are a mile out from shore. I look back. Parasailors drift high above the long stretch of white sandy beach. We try out various points of sail, tacking and jibing, each having a turn at the tiller.

Joelle goes over rules on the boat — how to hold the jib sheets and the mainsheet, shows us how to place our hand gently, not too tight on the tiller. She tells us where to place our hands as we tighten the winch and warns us to keep our fingers out of the way at all times. There are so many things to learn and relearn. So many new rules. The right way, the wrong way to do things. There is a beauty, a simplicity in how she holds all this — an attentiveness to what is right here.

As we turn with the wind now behind us, Joelle tells us to listen. Something there in the pitch of the boat, the sound as we turn this way and that in the wind. I can't hear anything except the wind and waves knocking the side of the boat. The boat heels. I clutch the side. Gulls fly around us. After a few hours, we turn to shore and motor back to dock.

"Red right returning," Joelle reminds us, "Keep the red markers on the right as we go in."

On land at last, sweaty and tired, I stumble off to the hotel, my legs rubbery, feeling like I'm still on board.

For dinner tonight I've found Nervous Nellies, a little seafood restaurant recommended by the hotel desk clerk a mile down the beach on the channel side of Fort Meyers. I find a table outside looking over the lagoon. I wear my new tan shorts and white linen shirt I'd bought in India the year before. The warmth of the sun has warmed me through. It's a beautiful night, early and not crowded on the deck, just a few other tables with friends meeting for dinner. I order a local Jai Lai IPA. Dave and I always ordered IPA's. He'd get one type, I'd get another. I always liked his best. The band, Left of Center, sets up across from me and beyond them in the lagoon, sailboats tied at dock, rock gently beneath a darkening sky.

Several weeks after our interview in Seattle, we learned that we were the search committee's top choice — but that there was a problem. The search committee had been charged with finding a senior pastor and an associate pastor but the senior pastor candidate had withdrawn at the last minute. The committee had to decide whether to wait for another senior candidate and then bring us all in for a vote together as they'd planned, or to vote on us alone now as their associate pastor candidate and then call a senior pastor later.

I asked the search committee chair if they'd consider me as senior pastor. She told me the church was dying to have a straight white male take over and indeed someone with more experience than my two years working in the church and running BE-HIV. The committee decided to bring Dave and me forward as their associate pastor candidates and ask the church to vote on us.

As the possibility of moving to Seattle became real I realized how much I didn't want to move. I wanted to stay in Chicago near Dave's brother, sister-in-law, and their amazing red-haired three-year-old son and baby daughter. And yet, Dave was depressed, had been for the past years here. It was a weight that I didn't know how to deal with so well, wanting it just to go away. I would come in too close — be too sexual, too physical, too in his face. Or failing that, when he pushed me away, got angry and mad myself, trying to get sadder than he was. To keep and find my own place and ground was hard and I failed at it often.

I remember one year, maybe around Thanksgiving. Thanksgiving was always hard for Dave, full of the memory of what he had enjoyed when he was a child — getting together with these other families to share the meal and play charades. That year, friends had invited us over. Dave couldn't go, didn't want to go. He couldn't get out of that dark, tearful, despairing, self-deprecating hole. I panicked at such times. Tried to do, did too much.

I went to their house alone. I remember — and this was rare for me — crying or being upset — this was a time before I really knew how to cry and was fearful that I didn't — I kept a lot of tears inside, wrapped up. I told them what was going on with Dave and about his depression. How hard it was, so very hard for him. What I hadn't acknowledged before was how hard it was for me. We played cards, Hearts, just the three of us that night. Life might be better in Seattle.

Here at dinner in Fort Meyers Beach, I pull out my journal,

"Today I went further out than I'd ever been before." "A mile out at sea. I was thrilled, ecstatic out there. This is what I came for. This. Why have I sailed into sad when there is so much more to see?"

I look around taking in the warmth, the sky, and the sailboats across, the memory of the day. Yes, for all of this I've come. I'm on my way.

"I sailed into sad when I came here yesterday and just about crashed and sunk my boat on that familiar shore. But today I discovered again that there is so much more. So many times I lost my point of sail and forgot which tack I was on. And today, I got reoriented, repositioned. I found my place on deck. I'm no longer just afraid. I'm something more — learning what is beyond my fear."

I introduce myself to the middle-aged bearded guy setting up the microphones for the band and tuning his guitar.

"How long have you been living down here?" I ask.

He tells me how back in Jersey, years ago now, he'd sat at a bar one night and saw across the room a reflection of a sailboat on the wall. He knew then and there that sailing was what he needed to do. He quit his job and headed down here so he could learn how to sail.

I remember the sailboat at the end of the pathway on my morning run in Portland a few weeks ago that reminded me that my journey didn't need to end in the despair of spinning on the regrets and second-guessing of the past choices I'd made.

As the band begins to play and the piano player riffs into a solo, I remember my piano lessons and learning how to improvise. I'd taken piano as a kid but only in learning improv had I ever really learned to listen to music, to really hear it instead of just pressing the keys. I loved the freedom to play over the keyboard and see what melody I might discover. My piano teacher had reminded me what Louis Armstrong had said: "There's no such thing as a wrong note, there's only a new opportunity."

When I learned to sail, I was so overwhelmed by all the new words, techniques, and skills that I never really thought about how sailing might take you anywhere. Today I've learned more about what boats can really do, where they might go and the rules to help you get there. I learned how to not be overwhelmed but to look for the signs that will help you wind your way out of the channel and back in. The possibilities open before me.

We flew out to Seattle a week before the congregation met to vote on calling us as associate pastors. The search committee had arranged for us to meet with small groups so the congregation could get to know us both. One night we answered questions in a forum in the packed sanctuary.

The search committee chair said that any questions deemed inappropriate would not be responded to.

The first question: "Our church has been reading Henri Nouwen's book *The Wounded Healer*. Could you reflect on your own experiences about the relationship between wounding and healing?"

Dave and I turned and smiled at each other. This was a lot better than being asked about our HIV status.

Others followed. "What do you think of people who quilt during church?" "How do you fight?" I told them what happened at the airport after we landed, and we got lost trying to find our way to my friend's house where we were staying.

On Sunday morning we woke early, anxious about how things might go. We'd split up the sermon. I preached the first part on fear and all the fears that could get in the way of heeding a call. Not knowing that Dave was going to speak next, a friend of ours told us afterwards that after I spoke, she'd put her head in her hands and shook her head. But then Dave came in with the second part and talked about courage in the face of fear. We ended with a quote from St. John of the Cross.

"I said to the man who stood at the gate, give me a light that I may see my way into the darkness!"

"Put out your hand into the hand of God" he said, "That will be a better light, and safer than a known way."

We waited at the house of members of the church while the congregation debated and voted. The search committee told us they hoped we'd come if we got more than the required 67%. It took an hour for the questions and to count the votes. And then we got word, the vote was in — we'd got 73% of the vote. The congregation had put out their hand into the dark, the uncertainty and unknown. The boat of possibility had turned out of irons, out of the no-go zone.

We walked into the sanctuary and the congregation was singing *Amazing Grace*. A young dad stood up and said that this was the kind of church where he wanted to raise his children and gave the church a check for $10,000. The press were waiting outside. The next day a serious picture of us in our ties was on the cover of *The Seattle Times* next to a picture of the first test flight of the Boeing 777. Dave looks confident. I look scared. My mother worried we might be killed.

We were the first gay couple called to a church anywhere and there was a flurry of newspaper articles around the country. It was our two minutes of fame and the church's groundbreaking decision. My favorite story was how the news went out on the BBC and got picked up by a church in Istanbul where the pastor heard it and lambasted in his sermon what a terrible thing this church in Seattle had done. A church member was a mission worker in Turkey and member of University Congregational. She told the pastor after worship, "That's my church!"

The senior pastor at a conservative megachurch in Seattle said our call was the most disgusting thing he'd ever heard. I thought he had a limited imagination. Later he was picked up for soliciting sex in men's toilets.

The former senior pastor of the church had been forced to resign after he'd had an affair with a member of the congregation. His ex-wife, Ruth, invited us to come see her house after the service. It was a beautiful cedar shingled house near the church with a beautiful garden in front and view of Lake Washington. We agreed to rent it and Ruth offered to give us much of her furniture as she was ready for a new chapter of life and to leave this old one behind. She promised that any bad vibes from her marriage had been cleansed away.

It was my idea to have a commitment service that summer in Chicago. I wanted us to have a service before we got to Seattle, before people in the congregation could fuss with why we didn't have a ceremony to mark our relationship. It felt like a rule that I wanted to have met before going. We'd been together eight years by then and had talked about having a commitment service before but we were holding out, waiting for the day that my folks might feel like they could possibly come.

Besides, it felt like good timing to plan the service for that summer. As we'd sent out invitations that spring we knew that there was the vote coming up in Seattle in June and we'd either be moving there or staying in Chicago. Either way we'd need our friends to support us. We'd be the first same sex wedding at St. Paul's United Church of Christ, the large gothic church in Lincoln Park, just north of the Loop in Chicago. We worried about how it would go over in this very established, traditional church built with Oscar Meyer money.

We told the associate pastor, that we wouldn't kiss during the service. Dave and I had talked about that and we were both uneasy about the thought of kissing in front of my parents. Instead, we'd hug. We planned to officiate at communion afterwards. Dave wrote the script like he always did and like I always did I didn't follow along too closely. I tried to but it just made me nervous and uptight. I did much better just looking up and out at the congregation and saying what was in my heart as best I remembered — even if I didn't get all the words right.

That Saturday morning for our commitment service we stood facing each other in our blue Brooks Brothers suits, welcomed our friends and families that had come. After sharing our vows, we hugged. It felt like we'd signed a contract, made a formal agreement, a business deal. And perhaps that is part of what we did — we were marking this new beginning as well — off to serve as pastors together.

On the first Sunday in Seattle, the interim pastor welcomed us to church.

"The powers that be put down a line in the sand," Bob said, "and this congregation walked over it."

The congregation erupted in cheers.

In Zen, the Ten Precepts are like the Ten Commandments — guidelines, as Genjo explains, that can help us point and find our way when we forget. "But there are times when it's right to break the precepts as well. It is important to discover what those times are," he advises.

"If you have a collision, both parties are at fault. So if the boat coming at you should be moving away according to the rules, no matter what the rules say, you need to stay out of the way even if you are right," Joelle reminds us.

Maybe I don't have to worry so much about following the rules in order to be 'right,' I think. Maybe I need to learn the rules in order to go somewhere out here, following the green and red markers, winding my way through, finding my way.

CHAPTER 10

Man Overboard

Livery Checkout: Complete the man overboard drill

It's Wednesday afternoon, our third day of sailing class here in Florida and a beautiful day out in the Gulf, a mile out from shore. The water is a brilliant blue, and the sky is dotted with white clouds.

Joelle tosses the red personal flotation device, otherwise known as a PFD, into the water. It lands with a hollow plop as the boat peels away. "Man overboard!" Joelle shouts. "Peter, keep your finger pointed at the cushion. Don't lose sight of it."

As the boat peels away it looks so small, forsaken out there rolling in the waves... *Where is it? I lost it already. Oh, its right there.*

Dave and I drove out to Seattle in early August. We marveled at signs for "Pacific" and "West Coast" wondering where in the world we were living. I found out here, so far from home, something I'd never expected. There was more air out here — I could breathe and was finally beginning to.

I was so struck by how people were different out here — they hugged instead of shook hands at coffee hour. They talked about intimate details of their lives in the greeting line after church — talked about things that in New England would never be spoken aloud.

We spent a lot of time looking around at coffee hour, wondering who might be in the 27% that hadn't voted for us. We reached out and tried to make a good impression especially on anyone who we thought might not have been supportive of our call. Time after time we judged folks wrong and instead of fear we were met with invitation — come to dinner! We had lots of dinners. Poignant conversations like with the man who worried that we might become a 'gay' church and others anxious about the morals we were teaching to their grandchildren.

Out on the boat Joelle tells us we need to fall off, head away from the PFD for six or seven boat lengths, then come up into the wind. I keep my finger on the PFD.

"Ready about!" Joelle shouts. We tack and head back. The PFD off to the starboard side of the boat. "When you see the PFD off the right front there — like at two on the clock — come up towards the cushion, and let out the sails in safety position to slow the boat."

My first visit was to a kind elderly woman, nearly 100, with bright white curly hair and a voice that quivered. She lived in a retirement community down the hill from the church. We had a nice visit I thought and then I rose to leave.

"I don't know much about gays," she said.

I sat down.

"What would you like to know?" I asked, worried about what I might have opened myself up for.

She paused.

"How do you cook?"

I paused, wondering what she meant.

"Well, there are things that Dave likes to cook and there are things that I like to cook. I like to make soup. He likes to make bread. He cooks sometimes, I cook sometimes."

"Oh," she said, "That's like what my grandson and his wife do — they share cooking."

On the boat, Joelle, brings us right up alongside the PFD, leans over and grabs it. Tosses it again. This time it's my turn to try to retrieve it.

"Man overboard!" I shout and take the helm.

Horace was a curmudgeonly old man who sat in the front pew below the pulpit and commented on sermons out loud. If you said something like 'needless to say' Horace would pipe up in his gravelly voice, "Then for God's sake why say it!" One day at the end of worship I followed him during the closing hymn to the back of the sanctuary. As the congregation hushed as the chimes rang one, two, three times, Horace pivoted on his walker, turned to me and exclaimed in his booming voice for the whole church to hear, "I don't think you two have done a damn bit of good since you've been here!"

Horace's outburst prompted me to set up a visit with him. He was dying, his wife had died a year before. Something happened in those visits. He opened up like that one day when he shared that he'd wanted to join a fraternity at the University of Virginia but wasn't allowed to because his grandfather was Jewish. He too knew how prejudice and bigotry had wounded his life. I officiated at his memorial service a month later.

I peel off away from the PFD counting boat lengths in my head and wondering how I'll find my way back to find the cushion. Bob and Judy have their fingers pointed. Together we may find our way back.

A year after Don, the senior minister of the church was called, he said we needed to reorganize ourselves as a ministry team. He recognized the gifts in ministry and preaching that our colleague Gail, Dave, and I brought and proposed that instead of hiring a new Christian Education Director to replace the Director who was retiring, that the four of us split up the responsibilities and hold that role as a team ourselves. Gail would work with preschool, me with elementary children, Dave with youth and the youth minister and Don with adult education. I moved to full time, Dave to 80% time. We each preached once a month. We made decisions as a team. Don said often, "Salvation is just around the corner." In the eleven years we worked together, we helped move the church a bit closer to deeper connections, reaching out to strangers, and healing old wounds of suspicion and betrayal.

After seven years at our house, Dave was ready to move into a more interesting and urban neighborhood. A gay couple was living with us and they were looking forward to having a child. We talked about buying a house together and heard about New Holly, a multi-class housing project being built on former housing properties. We toured the house with the carriage house in back above the garage, and I said yes, we could do this. I could do this. Dave and I would have our bedroom and study in the carriage house in the back.

On the morning we were to sign on the sale of the house, I walked with Dave down the hill across the street, sat on the curb and wept. Put my head in my hands and said I can't do this. I wanted to live upstairs in the new house. I wanted us to keep the house we were selling and rent it like a friend had told us we should do since he thought we'd regret moving and be coming back here. Dave got mad — said we had to move, we'd made a commitment. I just wanted empathy. *What was this about moving on that was so hard? What was I struggling to let go of?*

We moved to New Holly and Dave went on a buying spree and bought all of this gorgeous wood furniture from Stickley — really lovely stuff. He picked it all out. I loved our little carriage house where we could close the door. Several years later we went to go hide out there — cooking and eating our meals there on a little cardboard table — we'd given over the house to our housemates and their baby. They needed their own space and we needed ours. Life changed.

In 2004 we were asked to join with six other couples in a lawsuit challenging the legality of the Defense of Marriage Act that prohibited marriage between same-sex couples. There was a staged event on March 11, 2004 where we seven couples all stood in line to ask for marriage licenses and were turned away. There was something so heartbreaking about that day that was captured in the photo of us on the cover of *The Seattle Times*. My head on Dave's shoulder, his arm wrapped around me. He looks away over his other shoulder, his mouth half open.

There was something about all this that we did, we learned to do that was so heartbreaking — we got all dressed up, we stood in line, we polished our shoes, and none if it mattered — none of it. We were turned away. We'd played the game to find a place at the table, trying to get along, fit in and been turned away again and again. No matter how we looked, how polished our shoes were, how straight our ties, how neat our suits, we would never be allowed to get married. Two years later, the State Supreme Court ruled on July 27, 2006 in favor of the state. The Defense of Marriage Act was not overturned.

Out on the boat I come up towards the cushion but am too far away for Bob to lean over and grab it. I try again, come in too fast and run over it.

"One more try," Joelle encourages.

So I take one more turn and this time I head up a bit more into the wind, waiting long enough but not too long and the red float cushion is right there where it should be, just off the bow. We drift in safety position, the sails out, the boom over the water, the wind rushing through. We slow almost to a stop. I turn the boat a little bit away as Joelle leans out, grabs the cushion and pulls it aboard.

"Good job. Now let's try it again," and she tosses the cushion overboard one more time. As we pull away I have my finger pointing at the cushion tossing up and down in the waves, out of sight. *Where is it?*

One fall day, Dave and I stood at the edge of the dock on Alki Beach looking out over Puget Sound shrouded in fog. We couldn't see a thing — no sign of the rugged snow-capped Olympic Mountains that we knew were there rising above the Sound. Nothing out there but the moan of distant horns and a ferry moving in and out of the fog.

We'd been living in Seattle for ten years and it felt like a good time to move on. Dave was ready to move back to the Midwest, closer to his family, and a familiar landscape that he loved of cornfields and grain elevators where roads stretched clear ahead for mile after mile, never having to veer.

We'd seen and done so much together since we'd met in divinity school twenty years earlier. We'd supported each other in coming out to friends and family, learned to make a home together, went through a long search process for finding a church where we both could serve and made our own little moment of history. But now we were in a fog — with no clear road ahead. We needed, wanted different things.

A month later, Dave decided he was ready to move on from the church. I was just stepping into a new role as the youth minister at church. I was not ready to go. Dave wanted to work with folks who were poor and in a smaller church community. As a first step to getting there, he wanted to go to Guatemala and study Spanish. At first he was going for just a month. I encouraged

MAN OVERBOARD • 113

him to stay longer and really learn Spanish. I wonder now if I knew that I wanted this time alone too. He was off for three months, the longest amount of time he could imagine going. In seven weeks a couple of friends and I would fly down to see him.

As we prepared for Dave's departure from church that January, we preached intentionally about putting down the "Pete and Dave" story. We were "Pete and Dave" at church. People complimented me on things he did and complimented him on things I did. Half the church called me Dave. We were a third thing as a couple, a force, a presence. It had become another part of our our identity.

All of our life together had been about getting this position. All those years of doubting we could ever serve a church and be open together, the long search. Finding University was like finding the child we never had together. The church community was the child we reared together. We helped grow the church into its further maturity and development, and we grew as well in the process. Now that we both were not here at the church, who would we be? Friends asked if we were splitting up. Something was ending, but no, I couldn't believe it was the end of our relationship. I loved Dave and I needed different things that I found hard to claim.

At the end of Dave's last sermon at the church I crossed the chancel and went over to the pulpit and gave him a kiss. Dave took off his stole and a member came up and put it on him again at the conclusion of the service.

A few days later, I left Dave at the departures gate at Sea-Tac airport. A quick hug, furtive kiss. "Have a great time, do."

As I pulled out, I looked back. He was already gone. And then I began to do what I knew I was going to do the past weeks thinking about this day. I began to cry and didn't know when I would stop. So many tears and I didn't know why. For sure about Dave leaving but it was something more. Now that he was okay, more than okay, happy, maybe I could be as well.

A few weeks later when the tears hadn't slowed, I had lunch with Genjo and told him about this feeling that there was something behind me that was frightening but every time I turned to look at it I couldn't see anything there. He suggested psychoanalysis and I knew as clearly as when he had suggested I attend a meditation retreat years before that this is what I needed to do. It had been decades since the time at Yale when my therapist had talked about psychoanalysis. This time I said yes. I went to see Carter the next week expecting that I would get through whatever this was by the time Dave returned.

As I worked with Carter, something began to break open in me – my life, my heart, the possibility of my joy. And the joy came in part in an unexpected way, the welcoming into our home of a young man named Pedro.

Dave and I had talked about adopting a child in Chicago, but it wasn't legal for gay and lesbian couples to adopt a child in Illinois. When we moved to Seattle, we were surrounded by the gift of many children at church and we didn't know how with the demands of our work we could be parents in the ways we wanted to be. But offering support to a young man who could be independent, the young Guatemalan we'd heard about on vacation in Scotland who was seeking political asylum and needing a place to live after aging out of the foster care program, was something we could do.

I'd wondered what might happen with that guest room in our new condominium on Capitol Hill. Now I knew. The night after we arrived home a young woman came to the door with a thin, small boy, quiet, apprehensive — he looked about 14. The social worker told us that we should register him for school as soon as possible and recommended the Seattle Bilingual School. She said that as far as her agency was concerned, the case was closed and they were done with their responsibilities to care for Pedro in foster care. She wished us luck.

I went the next day with Pedro to register him for school. I said that I didn't want him at these other high schools — I wanted him to go to the Seattle Bilingual School. He got in. We signed up for soccer, got him a tutor at the resource fair. Made an appointment for him to see a doctor for a physical. That night I lay in bed feeling this love, the privilege of saying yes to this responsibility, this care, for the young man who was still such a young boy sleeping in the room next door. I didn't expect this.

A year later, Dave flew down to Guatemala to meet Pedro's parents and get his birth certificate — something he needed for his political asylum case. The next week Dave was off for two weeks at the language school where he had studied after leaving University Church.

Dave had asked me that spring what I would do if I could be happy because all that winter it was clear that I was not and neither was he. I said what I knew but didn't want to say, that to be happy I'd go get a place on my own, a little place to look out and see my life without even knowing exactly what that meant. All I knew was that I wanted some space, some time to ponder who I was, where I was going, who I was being called to be, and where I was called to go.

The day after Dave arrived in Guatemala he called and said he was seeking to re-create the past by coming down here, and that he didn't want to be there. He said he really heard me that I was sad and wanted to move out. He wanted to come home and put things together. He got Pedro's birth certificate from his family the next day and I arranged for a ticket for him to fly home. Coming home changed nothing.

The following spring after years of waiting, Pedro's asylum case came up. We didn't know what was best for Pedro — to go home or to stay here. He had his family in Guatemala, we had bought him land there for him to farm. On the day of his asylum hearing Pedro met with us right before the hearing began and said that his lawyers said that he was going to lose the case and the best scenario would be for him to apply for voluntary deportation — that way he could have a few months to say goodbye and fly home on his own terms. If he didn't he might be deported that very day. His lawyers said they wouldn't keep working with him if he wanted to continue to pursue the case. Pedro's application for voluntary deportation was accepted and we came home.

Sunday afternoon, a month later, I came home after church, opened the door to our condo and called out "Hello! I'm home!" Silence. Pedro's door was open, his room, empty. On the wall above the couch, pictures taped to the wall — friends on the soccer team, a banner from school and a painting he'd made of the profile of a young girl holding a rose with a tear running down her cheek. I sat on the couch, sobbed, called Dave. It was four months before we heard from him — on Thanksgiving night. The phone rang.

"Hello. This is Pedro...."

I held the phone and wept. He was okay. He'd found his way to Houston, was working in a restaurant. He was okay. Now maybe I could be too.

Out on the boat, as we head back to dock, we need to lower the sails.

"Peter! Douse the mainsail!"

I stand up and narrate my path, accenting every sailing term to instill it to memory.

"DOUSE the MAINSAIL means pull down the MAINSAIL. So I am now walking to the BOW and taking off the SHACKLE and releasing the HALYARD."

I look to the back of the boat, (that would be the STERN), where Joelle and my fellow students are holding their heads in their hands.

I'm sure that all week I've been narrating out loud in a booming voice my every move like they do on those TV cooking shows: "NOW I am adding a PINCH OF SALT and STIRRING!"

"DON'T THROW ME OVERBOARD UNTIL SATURDAY!" I laugh. The class ends on Friday. My boisterous narration of my every move is why our sailing instructor Joelle has named me "Mr. Parts of the Boat."

I don't know why, but I can't imagine making it through without talking it through. All these parts of the boat are so confusing and confounding. Truly, three months ago I barely knew the BOW from the STERN and PORT from STARBOARD.

If I don't say the parts OUT LOUD, I get them all messed up. The only way through I've figured out is to narrate my moves and name the parts, to hold these strange and wonderful words in my mouth and then try to remember what I'm supposed to do with them.

Perhaps someday I'll be a sailor who doesn't have to narrate his every move out loud, but that day feels a long way off.

Only a few months earlier I'd sat in that first sailing class, a little model of a sailboat in front of us, and practiced naming the parts of the boat out loud. The KEEL down under. The RUDDER and TILLER, the LEECH and the LUFF, the HEAD of the sail.... So many new words I'd learned this week — WINDEX and BOOMVANG, BOWSPRIT and BATTENS, FOOT and FORESTAY, FENDERS and the BITTER END.

The week before I flew down here for sailing school, I visited an elderly member of my congregation who had just been admitted to the hospital. I pulled a folding chair up close to his bedside and like I'd done at so many bedsides so many times before, recited the 23rd Psalm. "The Lord is my shepherd I shall not want..."

Maybe it was my imagination or perhaps just my hope, but I also think it was true, that as I recited those old words his breath settled and quieted. I felt a quieting myself in my own anxiety about the week coming up in Florida.

"Yea, though I walk through the valley of the shadow of death, I fear no evil, for you are with me, your rod and your staff they comfort me…." (Psalm 23:4)

We'd known each other twenty years, nurtured a regard, a respect and care for each other. Each Sunday we greeted each other in the back of the sanctuary before worship began, he with his red boutonniere that the ushers wore and his tie. He was reserved, cautious, about letting others in, walled himself off in a world of "fine." I understood. Slowly over time the walls melted between us, for both of us.

Now a stroke had left him silenced, immobile except for his darting bright blue eyes. His hands wound in white gauze to keep him from pulling his oxygen tube out. He'd had a massive stroke the day before and was not expected to live but for a few days.

I called his wife and held the phone close to his ear as she told him what she had told him each day for 68 years, "I love you, I love you. You've been the best."

His eyes focused, stilled, quieted. He looked out beyond the corners of the room as I remembered how we used to joke with one another about the wearing of ties, double Windsor knotted. We both used to wear ties all the time on Sunday mornings, then less and less, until finally, not at all.

Tonight at the little outdoor pub looking over the lagoon, I stumble over the new words in my mouth as I review the various parts of the boat and points of sail. I think of all the new words that have come into my life. A new street address, new friends. I know I need to add a new word, *divorced*, to my life so I can move forward. It's a word I don't want to learn to say, a word I don't want to have anything to do with me, and a word I can't yet say. I've learned to say *separated* or *living apart* but *divorced* has a sting to it, a finality that I can't bear embracing. I struggle over the what-if's and if-only's trying to figure out the missing piece that made the relationship with Dave no longer work for me. Part of me wants to go back to my fantasy of how it had been years before, to carry forward the history we'd made, the future we'd dreamed, the time together, all of it. The other part of me knows it had to stop in order for me to continue to grow into who I am becoming. All this past year I've narrated my way through my day:

"I'm getting up."

"I'm walking."

"I'm breathing."

"I'm okay."

"It's going to be all right."

These days, it's how I get through.

I remember today retrieving the float cushions Joelle tosses overboard. When I hear the lonely plop of the cushion on the water falling quickly away behind us I think of Dave, of everything that had been our life, of all I have lost. *Why can't I find my way back to who I was, who we were? And if I can't find my way back, can I make my way forward to the new life I feel calling me out? What do I need to die to and what can't I give up? What is the turning word I need to hear so I can stop clinging and let go?*

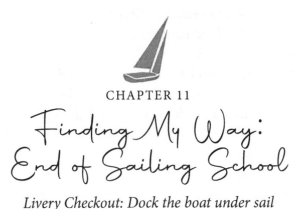

CHAPTER 11

Finding My Way: End of Sailing School

Livery Checkout: Dock the boat under sail

The last day of sailing school in Florida, I get up early and go for a long run down the beach. The night is just turning to dawn, the air cool, and sand damp, beach empty. The last stars fade into a sky slowly brightening. A line of gold glows in the east beneath a band of dark clouds. It's the time of a new chance emerging, a time of day when everything seems possible. Beside me the sea stretches out quiet and smooth, waves gently lapping the shore. I chase sandpipers scurrying up and down the beach. They run ahead, flutter off over the surf, land a bit further ahead, come back to play some more.

As I run, I know that I've come for this. Come to run along the shore in the morning rising light dodging the surf and chasing sandpipers. Come for this last morning zigzagging up and down the beach, dry sand to wet, in and out of the surf line, waiting for the sun to rise and cover the day in bright warm light.

A friend once told me that in times of deep grief in his life he had gone to the beach, followed the line of the waves as they flowed in and out, as he contemplated the loss, changes, ebb and flow of his life. A few years ago, I'd done that same ritual myself, out on Fourth Beach on the Olympic Peninsula. But this time is different.

Today, I run in exultation — the ebb and flow of tides no longer just about tracing loss but about discovering hidden gifts as well. I stoop to pick up pieces of driftwood, small shells. Yes, now when the tide is going out, just the time, the necessary time, to launch a boat.

I've come for all this and I don't want to go home. I want to learn and practice, perfecting what I'm just beginning to learn. I want to go out for one more day and talk my way through the parts of the boat. I want Joelle to show us one more time how to quick tack down the channel, eyes peeled for boats coming up and down. One more day to practice all the points of sail, to learn how to chart a course and use a spinnaker. I don't want to leave. I want one more day.

I remember the feeling over the past year, biking up to our condo on Capitol Hill and wanting to keep biking right by. I hadn't wanted to go home with Dave for months. I wanted a little place on a hill to look out and see my life. I tried and tried to climb the hill, couldn't get there. I loved Dave and I loved the life we had made, and our routines and patterns, and I was so bored with it all — so bored with living his life, his way. Loved taking care of him, worrying and fussing over him and his depression and never being happy with the way things were. And it was killing me too. My life was sparkling more and more away and outside of home, but at home it was so depressing.

Something was happening to me. My life was popping open. After twenty years, I bought a new rain jacket even though it cost more money than I'd ever spent on a rain jacket. I went to the gym and learned about working out, I loved sweating and working hard at the gym, I liked my body for the first time ever in my life — not fussing over my stomach or my hairy chest.

I looked good, felt better. I didn't know what to make of any of it. It was like I was trying on not only a new set of clothes but a new skin, inhabiting a deeper sense of myself. It was all very curious — exciting and off-putting at the same time and especially when I started to take notice of women. Who was this man that was interested in looking at women? Who liked who I was when I thought about dating, being with a woman? What was going on? What was happening to me?

As my sessions with Carter went on I discovered these two distinct parts of me — the part that wanted to stay in the familiar and be with Dave and the other part of me that wanted to step out and come to life in some ways that I couldn't in that relationship. Most mornings I went to sit at my Zen Buddhist community, and Dave and I no longer sat and had our morning prayer time together. Morning after morning I sat on my cushion at Zen and wrestled, tried to figure myself out. Finally, in the moments before the bell rang to mark the end of the sit, I'd breathe. Just breathe.

I talked with Carter about fitting in. I struggled with expressing why I felt like it no longer worked with Dave — worried and wondered what had gone wrong and what had changed in me. Carter said when people change, not all things fit like they once did.

But today is the last day of sailing school and I must leave. Later that morning is the multiple-choice test Joelle has prepped us for all week. As I fill in the little ovals next to my answers about rules of the road, right of way, and rigging the boat, I'm amazed at all I've learned. But one question about the parts of the boat stumps me. *What is the name of the line that controls the mainsail?* I picture myself as I walk around the boat saying the names aloud, but I can't find the word. That word, the word I need. What is it? *Mainline?* That sounds right — I color in the little dot.

Joelle passes out the exams. She hands me mine, looks disappointed. She's counted on me to ace the test, but alas it's the MAINSHEET not the MAINLINE that controls the MAINSAIL. Of course. It's a small matter, a wrong choice, but behind the little mistake, a bigger question. Do I undermine myself? Do I step away from the confidence I've learned in learning to sail? Joelle is right. I have what it takes to ace the test. I have the discipline, focus to do it. What might happen if I show all I know?

When I moved out of our condo, I felt so happy having my own apartment, my own space. This was so what I needed. And I moved back home with Dave three months later at Easter because it felt like an appropriate marker and I knew that if I stayed in my own place I'd start doing things I'd enjoy. I'd imagined I might start dating and perhaps a woman. I'd start having an independent life, and part of me was not ready for independence. So I moved home and when I did, I knew that within the first hours and days I was done — that I wanted something that I couldn't express, couldn't name, couldn't say. I wanted things I wasn't supposed to like: to be on my own, to be independent. For what? To discover my life. Months later, I moved out again.

This afternoon Bob, Judy and I are going out for our solo sail. All week I've fussed over the schedule for our last day. Why not use the last class for one more lesson, one more day to hone what we had just begun to learn? But no, instead we are off for a solo sail. What can I possibly learn from that? How are two more hours alone in the boat with Bob and Judy bickering going to teach me anything?

Joelle coaches us through our launch and then calls me over as she sends Judy and Bob off to rig the boat. She walks me back down the dock, pauses, looks me in the eye.

"You've learned a lot this week, Peter. You know your stuff and I'm counting on you to keep an eye on things. Don't be shy about sharing what you know."

I feel the dock under my feet. Feel the warmth of the sun on my arms and legs. I tilt back my hat, roll back my shoulders. I can't believe she is sure of me and my skills. She's proud of me, I think. No, I realize, that's me, proud of myself. I'm learning to sail. I know what I'm doing and I can't hide what I know. I've come a long way from that young guy yelling on the boat, scared that we were going to capsize and he's going to drown. The boat hasn't capsized and I haven't drowned.

As we head out, down the channel I hear this voice rising in me, a new voice I don't recognize as my own but one I realize I like,

"Help me bring in the fenders, Bob. Yes, just flip them up and place them here. Great!"

I imagine them rolling their eyes…Who asked "Mr. Chipper" on board?

"Watch where you're going Judy — Judy, watch that buoy…."

I find what I've been hiding for so long — my own confidence, my own voice. As we motor around the bend in the channel, I look back at Joelle waving in the distance. We turn out into the Gulf and a warm offshore breeze. As the sea opens before us, I see what I couldn't see before. This is what I've come for. This feeling, this accomplishment, this pride, this wonder at being out here, just the three of us novices, out here sailing alone. Whoever put this schedule together was right — this is the pinnacle experience of the week. We have what it takes to sail the boat. I knew we did. I knew I did.

"Are you ready to give this a try?" I ask. "Let's put it in neutral, Judy, and head up into the wind. The other way, Judy, the other way, with the wind at the bow — the bow — the front of the boat. Bob and I will raise the sail."

I'm standing out on the bow, clutching the mast while trying to unfurl the jib, the boat rocking in the Gulf, a mile from shore. As I raise the jib and it fills with wind I think, this is how I want my life to unfurl.

I've learned this all week at sailing school — how to get out here, out on the water and actually go somewhere. Perhaps someday I'll be able to navigate beyond shame and guilt, out past fear and failure. Perhaps someday, I'll learn to sail.

I've learned that I can tack into fear or can come about and turn to joy. I can pinch too tight or release and let the sails fill. Maybe yes, sailing school can actually teach me to go somewhere. I'm learning some new words to point my way forward. Narrating aloud, I'm learning to sail.

Out rocking in the waves in the Gulf, sails up, engine off, all I can hear is the lapping of the water against the boat, the wind fluttering the sails. I'm ready to play. I want to stand with my hand on the tiller, practice tacking, jibing, heading up, falling off, coming about. I want to call out commands, play with close hauled and beam reach, turn us in circles and circling again feeling and practicing all the points of sail. And yes, I want to head out towards the horizon, confident that I know how to get there.

Judy and Bob on the other hand want to drift. They stretch out, prop up their feet. "Let's just hang out here for a bit," they call, eyes closed. This is what they came for, the culmination of their week — some time out here on the water to rest and relax. I came to sail.

Hand on the tiller, I can't wipe the smile off my face at how happy I am to be out here in the Gulf of Mexico. I think, *Can you believe it! On a sailboat! Sailing a sailboat — me! Amazing!* My exuberance and Bob and Judy's complacency compromise. We agree to take turns captaining, shifting between rocking in the waves and practicing all we've learned like finding a point ahead and tacking our way to it.

I pay close attention when Bob is at the helm as we drift towards an inadvertent jibe. "Watch it, Bob! Watch! Watch! Don't let the wind come up any closer behind the boat — watch the boom! The boom! THE BOOM! YES! THAT! TILLER TO BOOM!" I cower, duck. Happily, this time, once again, we avoid doom.

Out here in the exhilaration of captaining, I hear what I haven't heard before. I feel that presence Joelle talked about. Here, in this immense openness, the blue and white of sea and sky, I take it all in — the flow of the wind and waves, the angle of the sun rippling off the water, the wind on my face, the fluttering of the tell-tales, the feel of the mainsheet in my hand. It takes a quieting and stilling to take in everything that is here. Holding to no single detail so there is room to take in everything. It's Zen, Zen in a boat. It's the most wonderful feeling of aliveness and peace.

One day, I'd asked Elena, "What do you love about sailing?"

"It's like a reset button," she said.

"What gets reset?" I asked.

She paused, looked at the rain shower spotting the windows of the livery.

"It restores my perspective. At the end of a workday, sailing takes my lingering anxiety down a notch. You can't think when you go sailing. You just sail, emptied of anxiety."

"Tell me," I asked, "when you empty out the anxiety, the stress, out there on the water, what comes in to meet you?"

"Nothing," she said, appearing surprised at the question. "Nothing comes in. It's just empty."

Now I understand what she meant. When I'm empty, I can notice things like the sound of the water on the hull, how it sounds different as I tack this way or that and how the boat feels when it's sailing the best it can. Nothing else is needed.

It's like the feeling that comes at the end of a weeklong meditation sesshin. After all the long hours, and routine patterns day after day, after all the noise knocking around in my head has quieted a bit there is room for this taking in of everything.

According to the instructions I was given at the start of our classes at the Center for Wooden Boats at the heart of navigating are three questions: Where am I? Where am I going? How do I get there?

Today, I know where I am — out here on a boat in the best place I can imagine being. I wasn't so sure where I was going, but today I know that sailing is taking me there. I feel like a character I didn't know but want to get to know better.

I remember reading,

"For the truth is that to sail, to even contemplate sailing calls for a fundamental faith in one's life." (Richard Bode, *First You Have to Row a Little Boat*, p. 76)

Like Bode, as a young man I'd often been aware only of the barriers between myself and my destination. Now I've nurtured enough confidence to name where I'm going and want to go. This week Joelle had us mark our sights on the buoy in the distance and practice getting there, tacking or jibing this way and that. She had us come up as close to the buoy as the wind allowed, come up close and around again. Now I'm practicing out here myself.

Finding my way on the water out here I've learned is not easy with the constancy of waves that relentlessly sweep the boat forward, back, sideways. "All is disorder kept under control only by your ability to navigate," Bode wrote. (*First You Have to Row a Little Boat*, p. 180).

At home, I'd chased the familiarity of sorrow and sadness. But out here I find there is a lot more room to tack to the new and unexplored. I learn to come about and tack to joy. I realize I have a choice.

I used to believe that I needed to direct my life to how God designed and that my life was best lived attuning my life to

God's "purposes" as if God was "out there" somewhere. Now as I look around I sense God not "out there" somewhere but present here, everywhere — in the wind, the sea, the gulls, and the boat, all of it. I'm no longer seeking to be directed by some external commands but am listening to the Spirit within and around me — to have it flow through me, have this be enough.

After what feels like far too soon, we need to head to dock. We lower the sails, start the motor. As Judy captains us in, Bob and I flake the mainsail. We practice folding the sail in neat folds, pulling the sail back towards the stern, even and taut. We tie the sail down tight. We've done it neater than ever and done it out here on the water as well. Joelle will be proud, I think. I'm proud of how we did out here with everything this afternoon.

I stand at the bow, my arm wrapped around the mast as we round the bend into the channel. Ahead I see Joelle waiting for us on the dock. We tumble the fenders off the side. I think of how we must look out here — so shipshape coming in. As we turn in and prepare to back into the dock, Judy revs the engine in reverse.

"Too fast, Judy, slow it down," Bob calls. She slows the motor but we are still coming in way too fast.

Joelle calls, "Put it into forward!"

Judy turns the crank up instead of down, reverse instead of forward. We roar backwards. I grab the mast as we crash into the dock.

Despite our mishap right in front of our teacher, we all pass. Joelle gives us our blue record books and basic keelboat certification from the American Sailing Association. I'm proud. Prouder than I've been since passing my checkout at the Center for Wooden Boats.

Joelle takes us out onto the thirty-foot cruiser docked beside us. It's another of the boats that belongs to the Colgate Sailing

School and used for another set of classes and certifications. I wondered when I came here if I might want to sail a boat like this as it's the kind of boat that was in my dream that got me out here sailing. We walk around admiring the shiny polished teak, fancy gadgetry, and instruments, the wonder of a wheel instead of a tiller. As I look down at our little boat rocking at the dock, I realize how I miss being down there, close to the water, able to feel the wind and the sea rocking the boat. Up here everything is so removed, so distant. This is not my boat I realize. Closer to the wind and waves, the spitting surf and the boom swinging overhead (albeit above my head!) is where I want to be.

"I can see you in Seattle, Peter, out racing one of those lasers," Joelle says, "there at the bow screaming into the wind, waves splashing and wind roaring over you."

I laugh. It's an image of myself I've never imagined. And yet, who knows? It might just be me.

Joelle invites me to meet her and a friend at a bar in downtown Fort Meyers that night. Waiting at the bus stop on my way I get a call from my friend Ross in Vermont. I haven't talked with him in months.

"Hey Ross, guess where I am?"

"Sailing school! You amaze me, Peter! What's next?"

I wonder too.

"It's 7 degrees up here."

"It's 81 down here."

Perhaps a new life awaits me.

I arrive downtown and find the bar. I'm early and grab a stool next to a potbellied man with silver hair and a cowboy hat. He notices my Center for Wooden Boats ball-cap and we talk about boats. He's a powerboat guy and goes on and on about what kind of engines his boats have and how fast they go and how much they cost. As he drones on I look across the bar at the group of women who have just come in. Flowing summer dresses and brown, red, and black hair. One of them, a woman with long dark hair is stunning, beautiful. I sit and notice the women's hands, her long fingers as she laughs and twirls her glass.

Who is this sitting here enjoying watching beautiful women across the bar? Who is this who imagines himself walking over and introducing himself? Who is this man who sits here and even thinks these things? Who is this feeling attractive in my white linen shirt, unbuttoned one button lower than usual?

I think of Aki. We'd met at our summer meditation retreat with my Zen community. She'd walked in late, the last one in after the rest of us were all sitting waiting to be served tea. She entered quickly, bowed. Someone jumped up to show her where to sit. She looked around to find her tea cup, smiled, when the woman next to her pointed it out there behind her.

I sat across from her all week and watched her — so quiet and strong, so serene and focused. She was the only person who was actually Japanese at our Japanese Zen practice. It was funny and touching that she didn't understand how to do a thing. I sat across from her at meals and instructed her when to bow and when to pick up her chopsticks, when to pick up the black bowls one at a time and how to wash them with a daikon pickle. There was something about the way she carried herself, this intensity, this energy. I couldn't take my eyes off her.

I take a sip of beer, look at my watch, Joelle should be here soon. Sure enough, Joelle and her friend Joe walk in, and we go to get a seat at a little table outside. As we order dinner, I feel so privileged to be here. *How did I get to come out for dinner and drinks with my sailing instructor? Who am I becoming?*

"What do you do back in Seattle?" Joelle asks.

I hesitate, resist being defined again by whatever it is people think about "ministers." I'm not sure I want her to know.

"What do you think I do?" I ask.

Joelle thinks I'm a dentist.

Joe thinks I sell insurance.

At last, I give in despite everything in me that doesn't want them to know. I feel full of becoming — more than I am and not quite sure of who I might yet be. I tell them,

"I'm in a profession that no one wants anyone to know for fear of what they will think."

Joe guesses right away.

Joelle says, "You're kidding. A minister? Really?"

I laugh as I remember that's what Aki had said a few months ago when she'd learned on the meditation retreat that I was a minister. She said she was a Christian too. She said she wanted to talk about how I could do such a thing as bow to the Buddha. I tell her that in giving myself to the ritual I've become a better Christian. The practice of Zen has made real the things we talk about in Christianity like resurrection and incarnation. Here, every time I sit, I practice resurrection as I have to let go of all I am holding on to and find out what is on the other side of letting go. Here, sitting, drinking tea, bowing, I experience incarnation.

She was the first and only friend in the zendo I ever invited over for lunch. After lunch I suggested a walk to the arboretum and all the time we walked through the gardens I just wanted to hold her hand. It was such a strong feeling and so surprising to me. She told me later that I probed, asked her lots of questions. She told me the only reason she answered all my questions about her divorce and how she recovered from it, about her family and feelings about coming to America and what she missed about Japan, was because I was a minister.

We became friends. I texted her to see if she was going for the Sunday-night zazen. If she wasn't going, I wasn't so interested in going myself. When she was going I'd ask if she was interested in going to get a beer afterwards. I realized I wanted to get through zazen so we could go and sit and have this time together. I realized I looked forward more to seeing her afterwards than going to zazen at all.

And here was the thing, sometimes when we sat there on the barstools, I wanted to reach over and put my arm around her. Sometimes the feeling was so strong. Sometimes I sat on my hand to prevent myself from doing this. I never said anything about this to her. I didn't know what to do with this myself. I wondered who this man was who liked imagining putting his arm around this woman at the stool beside him!

When I'd asked for directions to the bar downtown, the woman at the registration desk at the hotel mentioned that she too was going downtown that night and said she might see me down there. As I walk down the street past the other bars I'm scared and excited that I might run into her. I'm curious how much I want to meet her. I wonder why I hadn't swapped cell phone numbers with her. I call a taxi and take off for the hotel. No wild night on the town that night. Too bad.

On the ride home I realize how much I need some freedom and space to live into the discovery of who I am. I need some space and freedom from people making assumptions about me — about what I do and think and believe, about who I would like to get hooked up with at the bar and even that I might like to get hooked up with someone.

"You need to be the ocean or you'll be seasick every day," Leonard Cohen sang. I know I need that vast ocean of sea and sky and spaciousness around me like I've found here out in the Gulf. I'm learning how to sail. I want to spend some time out here in this empty expanse and learn how to trust it to take me somewhere.

A year and a half after attending my first Zen mediation retreat I joined the sangha or community of practitioners. It felt like something I needed to do, to take this next step. I wrote Genjo about my desire to join.

"I feel like I've come to the end of a journey and found a sailing ship here in the harbor. Aboard are people with strange clothing and customs. I know that to get to my next destination I need to take this journey with them as they head out to sea."

After I gave myself to the Buddha, the Dharma, and the Sangha, I was given a new name, "Shin Ke," "Profound Home." This past week I discovered more about being at home in myself. Perhaps it had been within me all along.

After the fun evening with Joelle, it is Saturday and I'm headed home. Today, as the plane takes off from Fort Meyers Beach, I look down at the sandy coastline disappearing below as the plane takes a wide loop over the Gulf. I spot a few ships, a few white sails below. The sea and landscape widen out and further out. I feel like I can see to the edges of the earth. I breathe it all in. I don't remember seeing anything before like this beauty here below.

I wonder, *Who will I be when I return home? Can I escape the confines of who others think I am or should be and live into the fullness and complexity of who I am? Can I do this? And if not, why not?*

I'm ready to try. I'm in a new space between sitting in sailing school and showing what I know. I've learned to hold a point of sail and sail to where I want to go. I look at my reflection in the bathroom mirror in my Center for Wooden Boats ball-cap, tan from the sun all week. No longer just a "student," I'm becoming a "sailor." I smile. Perhaps I am.

CHAPTER 12

Getting Off the Dock, Again

A month later and I'm standing on a dock on the other side of Lake Union from the Center of Wooden Boats. Going to sailing school in Florida is one thing, as is going on a winter meditation retreat. Both in some ways, a comfortable setting in which to learn and practice. But coming home is where it counts and today, this is where I am.

I pull my hood up tight over my wool cap, cocooning myself from the cold wind driven drizzle whipping up the dock from the south end of the lake. I turn my back and look towards the shore. Spindly branches reach for black clouds streaking beneath a canopy of gray sky. I don't want to be here — not on a day like this.

Something has come up at home, and our sailing instructor Doug can't meet us to go sailing this morning. The blue tarps covering the boat snap in the wind; the boat knocks fretfully on the side of the dock. My cell phone is nuzzled in my cap next to my ear. I struggle to hear him.

"Why don't you two just get out there? Why don't you go give it a try?" he insists.

"But...really Doug?" I interject. "Are you sure this is alright?"

We'd come down this morning to the other side of the

lake where Doug has invited us to use his boat. Doug's friend Andrew and I have never sailed it before. We've never gone out sailing without Doug.

I look out at the white-capped lake. No one is out there this morning. We are fools to go. We should go home.

"You'll be fine. Just fine," he insists.

"But…" I stammer. Before he can hear all my excuses about what I can't do, he butts in, "Go on. Give it a try."

Of course he says, "Go give it a try," he always says things like that. He's been sailing all his life. He knows his stuff. Andrew and I are two novices. Andrew is a young thirty-something who moved here to Seattle from L.A. last year to work for one of the startup dot coms on the other side of the lake. He wants to buy a boat and sail around the world. He's young, cocky, and reckless.

I'm not, none of it, especially on a day like this. I'm just back from Sailing School with my Basic Keelboat certificate hung in a little frame in my office. I've learned at least some of the rules of sailing and I know how to follow them. I miss all the confidence and excitement I'd felt a month earlier in Florida at sailing school. Where has it gone?

In the previous few months I've learned how to raise a sail and tie some knots. I've learned how to tack and jibe and use the tiller. But despite all I've learned, part of me is still afraid every time the sails catch a gust of wind and we rise high above the water. This will be one of those days of lots of heeling and tippy sailing.

Every time I stand on the dock and contemplate the step out onto a boat I became a little five-year-old boy again, back in the basement pool at the old YMCA. The room echoed with the shouts of the other kids splashing in the pool as I stood there alone at the edge. I didn't want to get in. I hated getting in — the cold slap of water, the sting of chlorine in my eyes and nose.

Whenever my head went underwater I kicked my feet and flailed my arms as fast as I could and fought my way to the side before my breath ran out.

One time at that YMCA pool, Debbie, the swim teacher, swam over and looked up at me sitting on the side of the pool. "It's nice in here today. It really is. Here, I'll help you," she said, holding out her arms. I looked at her large green eyes and her white swim cap. I looked down at the water. I rubbed my toes over the gray tiles.

Debbie looked over to Mom. "It's okay if he just wants to sit on the edge today and kick his feet in the water."

She swam away.

Sometimes Mom would push me in. Out I'd fly and then down, down. I'd open my eyes to hairless white legs, bulbous thighs and fat toes. I'd flail my arms, kick my feet as fast as I could to break the surface and splash quickly to grab the slippery tiles at the side of the pool.

Today, back on this dock, there is no one holding out her arms to help me in. There is no one behind me to push me out of my anxiety. It's me alone, scuffing my boots on the wooden dock.

Doug is still on the phone.

"The sail's in the cockpit," he reminds me.

I look over at the boat. Andrew is already stringing up the sail and waving for me to help.

The blue plastic sheets covering the boat flap furiously in the wind. The rocky shore and steep bank loom across the narrow channel.

"When you get out, remember to tack hard to port and then turn up into the lake. Have fun."

He hangs up.

I pull the phone out from under my wool hat and put it back in my rain jacket pocket. I zip the pocket shut.

I look over at Andrew. "He can't come. He says we could go give it a try but — "

"Great!" he says, "Let's go! Give me a hand out here."

I take off my glasses, spotted with rain. I pull out the white handkerchief that my father taught me to always carry with me. I wipe my glasses. The water pools in the corners of the frames. I put them on. Everything is foggy, distorted. I take them off and brush off the steam with my fingertips. I want to go home.

Doug's boat is bigger than any boat I've ever sailed. The channel narrower than any I've ever navigated.

This is no longer the Center for Wooden Boats where Elena sits on a little stool in the livery with little registers to check out our boats. There are no rescue boats around here. Nothing in fact that looks at all familiar. It's the other side of the lake and a different boat. It's the two of us here, alone.

"Come on!" he says.

I step on board. Together we figure out how to thread the sail onto the boom and mast. I wonder, *How will we get out of here? Won't we just get blown back to shore?* I look across the narrow channel. There is no room out there to turn before we'll hit the rocks on the other side.

"Andrew, we've got to walk the boat up to the end of the dock," I insist.

"We can get it out from here. I know we can," he says.

"No, no, let's walk it up to the end."

The wind picks up. Drizzle turns to steady thick rain. Dark clouds billow over the lake that are now streaked with gray sheets. White-capped waves knock the boat against the dock.

The next thing I know Andrew jumps onto the dock and grabs the bowline. I run behind, reaching for the ropes streaming behind that keep falling from my grasp.

I yell to Andrew, "This is crazy! We're in over our heads!"

The waves knock our boat again and again against the dock.

"Come on! Come on! Help me here!" he yells back and tosses the bow line to me as he steps aboard our boat and pushes away from the dock.

"What are you doing?" I cry.

"I'm getting us off this dock!" he shouts back.

I want to tie up here first, to look out and think things through like we learned to do in sailing class. I want to plan a course, anticipate our tack.

Andrew wants none of that.

"But…" I say.

"Jump in or I'm taking off by myself!" he shouts.

There is that moment. This moment. I hold the bow line coiled cold and wet in my hands, tethering the boat. I want to go home. I want to go back. Because even if it was sad, even if it was not where I knew I needed to be, at least it was familiar. It was home. And who promised that there was more than that? Why did I want more? What terrible urge called me to set out into this fearful place — out of the comfort I had made of life into the discovery of who I was growing to be? Who said that's okay? Who said that's good?

Perhaps part of me will always be standing there on the dock with the boat tethered in my hands. Part of me will always be standing by the side of the pool not wanting to get in. Part of me will always be standing with Dave on a dock on a foggy day longing for something, anything, to see that wasn't what I saw — the need to discover my life.

And what the hell's out here, I think, but white-caps and wind and a boat we've never sailed and danger everywhere?

Andrew is sitting in the boat, hand on the tiller, ready to cast off. He looks up at me, wide-eyed, hopeful. I see that kid who jumps in the water without knowing how he will rise to the surface but trusting that he will.

"Go ahead, give it a try," I remember Doug saying.

"Come on!" cries Andrew, "Let's go!"

"I want you to be happy," the last thing Dave said when we'd last spoken, months before.

And a voice I didn't recognize — at least not at first, my own. "I want to go."

I toss the rope to Andrew.

I step on board.

CHAPTER 13

Sailing

A few weeks later, fifty degrees and pouring rain from thick
gray clouds that rest like a great wool blanket over the
city. A good day to cuddle up under a warm coverlet with a
good book and a cup of hot tea.

But out on Lake Union a lone sailboat is bobbing up and
down in a white-cap sea, heading up into a brisk north wind
and sheets of cold rain.

The solitary sailor tacks steadily through the wind side to
side. His little boat swings back and forth in the waves. Who is
this out here? Who would be out here on a day like this? Who
is this man out here — so full of joy, no place he'd rather be?

I imagine myself looking down from St. Mark's Cathedral
on Capitol Hill at that boat on the lake. Then, I see myself
beside him in his little boat. I feel the strain in his back and
arms as he pulls the mainsheet tight. I feel his hand rest on the
cold wet tiller and push it across as he tacks through the wind.
I feel the pull in his legs as he rises in the boat as the wind
whips the boom to the other side.

As he pulls the tiller across and lets out the mainsail, I realize
the stranger in the boat is me. It's me out here, red wool cap
pulled down tight, green rain jacket hood tied snug overhead.
It's me pulling the mainsheet and jib sheets strong and still,

moving side to side in the boat as the boom flies overhead. It's a dance, and me so happy, so free.

I'm learning to know, love and trust this man who is finding his life in a place he never expected, in a little wooden boat on a stormy day far from shore.

Now, out here on the water I feel it. Something I've never felt the same way out here on the lake. Such peace. Such incredible peace like I felt on that last day sailing with Bob and Judy in Florida. I would have to work hard to find all those things I was so stressed and worried about on shore.

I look back at the Seattle skyline moving in and out of sheets of rain through glasses spotted with rain. I count eleven cranes today. The city is changing. I'm changing. I'm figuring it out. I hear the voices of my instructors:

I hear Dick, "Hold your course."

And Charles, "Don't pinch, let out the sail."

Joelle, "Bring the tiller slow across."

And hey, Doug, I do. *I feel it.*

It's that "empty" you told me about Elena, and all those mistakes that I've learned from that have brought me here.

I feel it.

I hold the tiller gently, draw it steadily through the water.

"That's right," they all say, "That's it."

The boat turns, the sails fill.

I jump side to side tacking into the wind.

Epilogue

Years later now, I've taken over a hundred members of my church out sailing. There is something about this experience of stepping off the dock time and again, the conversation that opens up, the encouraging another to sail that that I want more of in my life.

Five years after my first sailing lesson, I write a letter to the church letting them know that I am setting sail from my pastorate to a new chapter in my life, beginning again. Late afternoon December 30, 2018, my last day as pastor at University Congregational United Church of Christ in Seattle. I've taken down from my office walls the map of Puget Sound, the faded construction paper sailboats that the congregation had made to celebrate my 20th anniversary here, a photograph looking straight up at a mast and a white sail unfurled in a blue sky. This morning I've taken off the church's white Christmas stole with a star and a wiseman and put on a bright blue stole given to me by a member of the church with a painting of a sailboat, its sails open wide to the wind.

It's my 25th year serving as pastor here, almost half my life and I am stepping out into a season full of unknown. All I know is that I need this time. Time to listen to where I am being called by the Spirit to go.

Its taken me years to get to this place of saying goodbye to a congregation I deeply love and that has walked with me through decades of growth and change. Not an easy journey through saying goodbye but ultimately a good one and I've navigated as well as I could. In doing so, I get the chance again to fall out of who I've been and into who I am becoming.

Likewise, I've been struggling over this book for years trying to get it 'right.' To wrestle to the ground what this story means.

"Stop trying to make sense of it all," my friends share, "And cut the preaching! Just tell the story."

I wanted to tell another story, a story I could be proud of. A story about doing it all perfectly and how things worked out so well. But I haven't led a perfect life and I'm far from a perfect sailor. I've also come to realize, with a good deal of fuss and reluctance, that perfection is an impossible ideal and a life lived with integrity and told honestly and vulnerably is what matters most. So here is my story — imperfect and incomplete. I'm still continuing to learn to sail.

As I make these final edits today, we are months into the COVID-19 pandemic that has swept the lives that we knew away. The disorientation I felt learning to sail is the disorientation many of us feel today. The uncertainty I felt not knowing if there was life on the other side of leaving the dock is an uncertainty we all feel. But I also bear witness to this hope: that as I found my way, we all will find ours. It's time for all of us to step off the dock and learn to sail.

Acknowledgements

This book could never have come into being without my incredible sailing instructors — Elena, Dick, Charles, Doug, and Kristin at the Center for Wooden Boats in Seattle, and Joelle at the Colgate Sailing School in Fort Meyers. Elena once told me that people who come to the Center for Wooden Boats stay for as long as they need in order to find out what they are looking for. Thank you all for helping me time and again to step off the dock and learn how to sail.

Thank you to my other sailing instructors as well — Tony Pane, Richard Carter, Rikki Riccard, Genjo Marinello, my colleagues and the members and friends of University Congregational Church in Seattle, my Dharma sisters and brothers at Cho Bo Ji.

Thank you to all my teachers and readers who helped me tell this story:

My teachers at Hugo House in Seattle — Theo Nestor, Emily Ware, and Carolyne Wright.

Laurel Rayburn who taught me to write sentences.

Greg Sletteland, my first reader and editor who told me there is a story here and encouraged me to tell it.

Kim Stafford who told me not to clean it all up and have it make "sense" and to my classmates and friends in the writing group, Esther Elizabeth, Dale Stitt, Kirby Lauderdale, and Linda Fisher.

My poetry writing group — Carl Woestwin, Marcia Rutan, Barbara Johnstone, Sheryl Shapiro, and Heidi Denkers.

Thank you to the staff and friends at The Seattle Folio Athenaeum who kept me faithful to the work — Lillian Dabney, Thula Weisle, Caroline Cumming, and David Brewster.

Thank you to Jennifer McCord for helping me get this book off the computer and out the door.

Thank you to Rudy, Roberta and Nathan for book design and line editing.

Grateful beyond words to Dave, Aki, my parents, sister Nancy, Thomas, Peter, Anna, Pedro and so many family members and friends who have taught me so much about the ways of love.

And to all my readers, a blessing with which I have concluded all my worship services since learning to sail:

May God grant you the grace never to sell yourself short.

Grace to risk something big for the sake of something good.

Grace to remember that the world is now too dangerous for anything but truth.

And too small for anything but love.

—William Sloane Coffin Jr.

About the Author

For 33 years Peter Ilgenfritz has served as a pastor in the United Church of Christ. A native of Massachusetts, he served for 25 years as pastor at University Congregational Church in Seattle before following a call to walk with others through times of change and transition. Peter is a member of Cho Bo Ji, a Rinzai Zen community in Seattle and a graduate of Colgate University and Yale Divinity School. Peter loves running, biking, conversations and writing. His book of poetry, *Setting Sail*, is available through Lulu Press. For more information on his ministry of coaching, spiritual accompaniment and retreat leadership contact him at *Peter@navigatingthroughchange. com.* or through his website, *NavigatingThroughChange.com.* Peter currently serves as interim pastor at the Congregational Church of Boothbay Harbor, Maine.

CPSIA information can be obtained
at www.ICGtesting.com
Printed in the USA
BVHW031642070421
604327BV00016B/280